GENE RODDENBERRY
THE LAST CONVERSATION

GENE RODDENBERRY

THE LAST CONVERSATION

A Dialogue with the Creator of *Star Trek* ®

YVONNE FERN

Foreword by Arthur C. Clarke

POCKET BOOKS
New York   London   Toronto   Sydney   Tokyo   Singapore

An Original Publication of POCKET BOOKS

POCKET BOOKS, a division of Simon & Schuster Inc.
1230 Avenue of the Americas, New York, NY 10020

Published by arrangement with University of California Press

ISBN: 0-671-52299-X

First Pocket Books trade paperback printing September 1996

10   9   8   7   6   5   4   3   2   1

GENE
RODDENBERRY
THE LAST CONVERSATION

Contents

. . .

Foreword

. . .

Although Yvonne Fern met Gene Roddenberry toward the end of his life, it is obvious that she got to know him very well indeed. I am delighted that she has written such a perceptive book about him.

Few men have left a finer legacy than Gene Roddenberry. At a dark time in human history, *Star Trek* promoted the then unpopular ideals of tolerance for differing cultures, and respect for all life-forms—without preaching and always with a saving sense of humor. We can all rejoice that Gene achieved professional success and world respect. There is a sad irony in the fact that he entered the Undiscovered Country just when the eagerly awaited movie of that name was about to be released, but it gives me great satisfaction that he lived to see so many of his ideals triumphantly accepted.

Gene and I had a warm relationship for more than twenty years, and I wish Yvonne's thoughtful portrait of Gene

Roddenberry all the success it deserves. I'm sure this will be guaranteed by the legions of intelligent people who will want to read it.

—*Arthur C. Clarke*
Sri Lanka
October 18, 1993

Author's Preface
to the Pocket Books Edition

. . .

In 1995, when I was giving a lecture at the University of California on an entirely unrelated subject, a man walked up to me and asked if I was the author of *Gene Roddenberry: The Last Conversation.* When I answered yes, he said, "Were you on drugs?" I laughed and asked him why. His reply was, "Gene Roddenberry was the biggest fraud that ever lived." He added, "I heard he died a few years ago."

"Yes," I replied.

"I hope he suffered," said the man—and walked away.

It turned out that he was a very prominent writer who had worked closely with Gene Roddenberry in the late 1970s.

It also turned out that since I wrote this book, I have heard that sentiment repeated, usually in less vicious terms, but with the same rancor, over and over—far too many times to attribute it to one jealous person here, one crank there.

All of these people are respectable, talented, and prominent in a variety of fields—writers, executives, directors, musicians, producers, etc. Many of them are also more well known, and more powerful in the entertainment industry, outside *Star Trek*, than Gene Roddenberry ever was.

But I remember the gentle, courteous, cooperative old man with whom I spent weeks and weeks, with whom I talked at length, for whom I truly cared, and I wonder if *they* are all on drugs.

Each person substantiates his or her story with irrefutable evidence. I read the hundreds of fan letters I received about the book, recall the devotion the fans have expressed toward Gene Roddenberry, the commendations and awards he has received, the warm approbation of his friends.

Dilemma.

I meet, fall in love with, marry Herbert F. Solow, the former head of Desilu, executive in charge of production for *Star Trek*, who made the *Star Trek* development deal with Gene Roddenberry, who sold the idea to NBC, who hired and worked closely with Gene Roddenberry before anyone else was on board. And I become privy to the memos, memories, stories, photos, letters, contracts, and reminiscences of a great many other people who knew and worked with Gene Roddenberry—from NBC executives to assistants in wardrobe.

Dilemma.

I read my own books again, only to see that (as one example) Gene says he laid out the bridge design for the *Enterprise*. I go to my tapes to listen to that part of the recorded interview to see if Gene even once mentions Matt Jefferies, who actually did design the whole thing with some input from Gene and Herb. He does not. I look at Matt

Jefferies's original sketches of the bridge, scores of them, in various stages of evolution, laid out on my desk in preparation for the *Star Trek Sketchbook* that my husband and I are writing. Perhaps Gene was mistaken . . . his memory failed him . . . he didn't mean . . .

I begin to believe that my book is fraudulent.

Dilemma.

I get a call from HarperCollins in England, who tell me they are just about sold out of the British edition of this book, there entitled *Inside the Mind of Gene Roddenberry*.

I feel worse.

Kevin Ryan, the senior editor at Simon & Schuster/ Pocket Books who purchased the paperback rights from the University of California Press, calls; he wants an *expanded* edition of my original book—for the new American edition. He asks me *to update the old material.*

Now faced with a practical dilemma, what do I do?

Refute those things Gene said that I now know to be untrue? Write a new book? Get into the swamp of dirt bios and trash the man who, with his wife, opened their home and their hearts to me?

Be honest? What *is* honest?

Honest in this case is that my 1991 experience of a dying Gene Roddenberry is as valid as the experiences of every one of those people. Most of them (though not all) had not seen him for at least twenty years.

I cannot say they were wrong.

They obviously were not.

Nor was I.

Therefore, the manuscript from which this edition is published is the original one—submitted to the hardcover publishers *before their editing process.* It recounts, as its title indicates, the extended conversation Gene and I had in the last year of his life.

It includes conversations and narrative that were edited out of the hardcover version, as well as some editorial transposition of sections or paragraphs. Additional comments and footnotes have been added to update statistics or clarify particular passages.

In the last three years, I have lectured on various subjects at various institutions, universities, and *Star Trek* conventions around the country. I am often asked to comment on certain aspects of my association with Gene Roddenberry; what *really* happened when Gene had his stroke, for example (since I was the only one there—besides the driver of the car). William Shatner's ghostwriter even called to ask about it so that he could write about it in *Star Trek Memories* (although how it could be a "memory" of William Shatner, I don't know). I have been asked if I would comment on Rick Berman's relationship with Gene, the Roddenberry estate, Majel's personal life, the contents of Gene's files, and a good many other subjects. I give the same answer to everyone, from Mr. Shatner's ghostwriter to television interviewers, columnists, and audiences:

No.

Yvonne Fern
Malibu
1996

P.S. Shatner wrote about it anyway!

GENE
RODDENBERRY
THE LAST CONVERSATION

Prologue

. . .

The phenomenon of *Star Trek* owes its origin to Gene Roddenberry, creator, producer, and unwitting catalyst of the future. Gene Roddenberry was a man of dreams—hailed as a genius by some (regarded as a fraud by others)—who talked with presidents, astronauts, physicists, and scholars but listened to his fans. He held in his hands a fictional universe called "the future," a place of ideas, full of wonders yet unknown, where it was possible for the human race to grow. It came to be called *Star Trek*.

Star Trek has always had two meanings: one is the title of a television show; the other is the philosophy incorporated into it. It, too is a place of ideas, chief among which is a belief in the essential goodness of humanity.

"If there was one theme in all of *Star Trek*," Gene Roddenberry was known to remark often, "it was that the glory of the universe is its infinite combinations of diversity. That all beauty comes from diversity. What a terrible, boring world it would be if everyone agreed with everyone else. When we are truly wise—and my test for a wise human is when they take a positive delight when someone says, 'I disagree with you because . . .'—my God, what an opportunity that will open!"

.   .   .

For every television show there is an audience, whether it numbers one hundred or one million. In the case of *Star Trek* and its spin-offs, the numbers are virtually uncountable, not because there are no statistics, but because *Star Trek*[1] is more than a television show.

At the death of Gene Roddenberry in 1991, letters from around the world were delivered to his widow, Majel Barrett, in boxes—for months afterward. There was one common theme: "*Star Trek* changed my life." It is, perhaps, the wondrous *personal* future *Star Trek* represents—its celebration of the human journey, its belief in the human spirit, and its message of love and tolerance for all life-forms—that remains unequaled by any television program today.

.   .   .

Star Trek has been incorporated into the American culture gradually since 1966. At first, its devotees were dubbed a subculture by the media. That is no longer true. Nor is it true that all devotees are "Trekkies"—or "Trekkers," as they prefer to be called. *Star Trek* was and is watched and admired by business, education and religious leaders, scientists, astronomers, astronauts, professors, teachers, corporate executives, artists, musicians, writers, doctors, parents, students, children, and government leaders, including presidents of the United States.

---

[1]Following convention, I use *Star Trek* to refer to the television programs, both the original series (1966–69) and its subsequent incarnations. Star Trek, without italics, refers to the philosophy incorporated in the shows and to the cultural phenomenon they engendered.

2

Star Trek actually consists of seven separate entities. The original *Star Trek* television series premiered on television on September 8, 1966, and was canceled three years later. The second *Star Trek* is a collection of twenty-two animated *Star Trek* episodes. The third *Star Trek* consists of six movies (to date) featuring the original cast. The fourth entity is *Star Trek: The Next Generation*, which began in 1986 and ended in 1995 and is now (as of this writing) a product of the big screen, with its own future in films (as of this writing, the second is in progress) ahead. The fifth is called *Star Trek: Deep Space Nine*. It continues the legacy of *Star Trek*, but is not Gene Roddenberry's original creation. The sixth is *Star Trek: Voyager*, the newest incarnation of the saga. The seventh Star Trek entity is the philosophy of *Star Trek*, which anyone who has examined the others will be able to explain. The world of Star Trek is composed of these major entities, together with a series of clubs, organizations, fan conventions, "fanzines" (amateur magazines produced by and circulated among fans), merchandise, and monthly mass-market publications (novels, official fan-club magazines, as well as serious studies examining the meaning of each episode, technical manuals, and much, much more).

■ ■ ■

You may not have watched *Star Trek* on television, but if you have been to NASA or seen a space shuttle flight or used a cellular telephone, you will have encountered it in real life. Many scientists, astronauts, engineers, and others attribute their inspiration, perseverance, and success to the influence of *Star Trek*. You have experienced it if you have been in the hospital recently, where medical computers monitor bodily functions, a development that, some say, is a direct result of Dr. McCoy's "bio-comps," seen in the original *Star Trek*. NASA developed the concept, which was first introduced to a mass audience as part of the everyday equipment aboard the *Starship Enterprise.*

In fact, NASA's first space shuttle was the precursor of that starship that isn't built yet. If you've ever seen it, you've seen the restraint of chronological time lose some of its grip on the future. People from around the country wrote to President Gerald Ford to ask that the prototype shuttle be named *Enterprise.*

If you have seen the Emmy Awards, *Saturday Night Live,* or any number of television shows that make reference to the inheritance of *Star Trek* as a cultural phenomenon, you have felt its presence.

Or perhaps you sometimes catch the tail end of "real-life" shows, like *Cops,* while waiting for the evening news. If you do, you may see a police officer make an arrest, as I did once. "Where's your partner?" he asked. "Here," the suspect replied. "Whaddya mean, here?" the policeman replied. "He was on the other side of town a couple of minutes ago. What did he do? Beam down from the *Enterprise?*"

．　■　■

In the Smithsonian Institution, you may have seen a mythical starship, displayed as though it existed, next to the historical biplane of Orville and Wilbur Wright and Charles Lindbergh's *Spirit of St. Louis.* If you were there in 1992, you would have seen an extensive *Star Trek* exhibition, a display of what has come to be known as contemporary American mythology that increased visitation by twenty-five percent in the year it was there. And, had you been quick enough to purchase tickets in the first few hours of their availability, you could have attended a symposium on *Star Trek* in Washington, D.C., the same year.

When the Smithsonian Institution mounted that *Star Trek* exhibition in the National Air and Space Museum, it was acknowledging a fact that millions of people have known for years: *Star Trek* is a significant influence in American culture. It is a legend, an adventure, a philosophy, a dream.

■   ■   ■

If you walk down Hollywood Boulevard, there will be, among the sidewalk stars of the screen giants of our film culture, one named Gene Roddenberry, the first television writer, curiously, to be so honored—as a result of the recommendations of the legions of *Star Trek* faithful.

And if you are a person whose eyes are drawn magnetically to the night sky, then you may see among the billions of stars in the cosmos one designated "Roddenberry" by the International Astronomical Union, in memory of a man whose series inspired thousands of people to reach for them.

■   ■   ■

Your computer originally may have been designed by a *Star Trek* viewer of thirty years ago who was inspired by the voice-activated computer on the *Enterprise* and decided to enter the future.

Your doctor may have gone into medicine because of Dr. McCoy. Your neighbor, son, daughter, brother, sister, parent, friend, may have been encouraged—not to follow a particular profession represented on the program, but to explore his or her own talents, and develop them to the private, particular, internal standard of satisfaction that *Star Trek* advocates.

If you thumb through a few university catalogues, you will see, among the philosophy and American studies classes listed, several dealing with the cultural icon of *Star Trek.*

Had you been to the Congressional Arts Caucus in Washington, D.C., in 1992, you would have heard an address on *Star Trek* given by Majel Barrett Roddenberry, Gene's widow. From the early '70s to the early '90s, you would have had the opportunity to hear Gene Roddenberry himself lecture at an enormous variety of institutions, from the Library of Congress to almost every major university and many minor colleges in this country. And if instead, you had decided to attend one of Dr. Isaac Asimov's lectures, you would have heard him say that *Star Trek* was the only television program he watched.

If, on the other hand, you are "not into" science fiction and prefer the more spiritual pursuits of Eastern philosophy, you might have had to wait patiently on the *Star Trek: The Next Generation* set, with your fellow monks from the Tibetan Dalai Lama's monastery in India, while they watched transfixed, as their spiritual leader's favorite television show came to life.

■   ■   ■

Star Trek is not just a property of America—it is a global commodity and a universal philosophy. Seen in over two hundred countries, translated into over forty languages, it is now an influence on planet Earth that cannot be ignored. As a tourist in England, you may have opened the British telephone book, in which there is an advertisement to customers, encouraging businesses to print their names in bold type. The advertisement reads: Boldly Go. It cites an example: **KIRK, ADMIRAL, JAMES T. SPC. EXPLR.** It adds that every enterprise needs a little assistance. There is no picture of the *Enterprise*, no logo, no Spock. It is assumed, throughout the world, that any reference to *Star Trek* will be understood.

If you read *Gulliver's Travels*, you hold in your hands the progenitor of *Star Trek*, which, as Gene Roddenberry said, "you can read as a child, and see a marvelous fairy tale of a giant and little people. When you reread it as an adult, you discover that it is a remarkable critical comment on the religious and political systems of the time."

This may have had something to do with the decision of President Ronald Reagan to visit the *Star Trek: The Next*

Generation set in April 1991. Or it might not have. Perhaps he was, like so many senators, judges, political colleagues, fellow actors, and friends, just a fan.

■ ■ ■

Because *Star Trek* was one of the earliest TV shows to incorporate a black female as a principal (in this case, an officer on the bridge of the *Enterprise*), you may have heard about Dr. Martin Luther King Jr.'s comment on *Star Trek* to Nichelle Nichols (Lieutenant Uhura on the Original Series): "You have opened a door that can never be closed again. Because of you and the way you portray the character, people will see us. The world will see us as we should be seen— men and women on an equal basis going where no one has gone before."

■ ■ ■

It is likely that sometime in the checkout lines at your local supermarket you would have seen the cover of *Newsweek* showing Spock's face, the cover of *Omni* featuring the *Enterprise*, and *People* magazine with articles about Gene Roddenberry or the cast and crews of the series, as well as several issues of *TV Guide* depicting some aspect of the *Star Trek* world (not to mention the tabloids). If you subscribe to other kinds of magazines, perhaps you came across the article in *Penthouse* in 1976 in which Gene Roddenberry was interviewed—about television, God, and the human condition; or you may have seen innumerable other publications in which, since 1966, the magic of *Star Trek* has been explored.

Walking through any toy store, you will inevitably come upon action figures, model ships, and communicators, all from the *Star Trek* series. Hallmark stores carry dozens of greeting cards with the faces of the *Enterprise* crews and even tiny *Enterprise* Christmas ornaments with workable lights. If you decide to do your Christmas shopping by catalogue, you will find it virtually impossible to avoid the hundreds of *Star Trek* items available, from uniform patterns to sweatshirts to mugs. Art galleries across the country now display what has come to be known as a new genre, "*Star Trek* art," from such genre artists as Michael David Ward and Keith Birdsong.

And if computers are part of your life, there is a surprising array of *Star Trek* software to be found, from games to screen savers to educational programs. If you prefer to browse quietly through a bookstore, you will find shelves of *Star Trek* books, from novels (Pocket Books publishes approximately four a month; to date over thirty million have been sold—the best-selling series in publishing history) to technical manuals that specify the physical properties and propulsion systems of the *Enterprise*.

These are but a fraction of the ways in which you will have watched *Star Trek*, simply by living in the twentieth century. But beyond greeting cards and toys, beyond advertising and merchandise, you will have watched *Star Trek*, even if you have never seen it on television, if you've ever known someone who does.

You will have seen *Star Trek* if you go to church or synagogue and your priest, rabbi, or minister says, "Love thy neighbor."

■　■　■

If you *view Star Trek*, the Original Series, you will see a lot of orange paint, plastic plants, a pointy-eared guy named Spock, and a collection of rubbery aliens. If you *see* it, you will see questions, and very few answers. How can we overcome prejudice? What is death? Should we orchestrate war? Is patriotism a disease? What is the difference between sexuality and love? When does duty end and morality begin? Should there be government? Whose ethics predominate in a relationship—mine or yours? And most often: What does it mean to be human?

If you *view* the three subsequent *Star Trek* incarnations, you will see great special effects, terrific makeup, and astounding technology. If you *see* it, you will see the same questions—explored in greater detail, with additional concerns that our current society engenders: Do machines live? What use is religion? Is love the exclusive property of heterosexuals? Just because we *can* do something, *should* we? What is the difference between dreams and reality? What is consciousness? Is there a case for drug dependency? What is the difference between male and female power? Are ethics the same as morals? And again, most often: What does it mean to be human?

And if it seems silly to imply so much from a commercial television show whose purpose is neither to entertain nor to impart philosophy, but to make money, you can read what Gene Roddenberry had to say about that. This is not a biography. This is a recorded conversation about ideas with a man whose series became an ideology, on screen and in what is fondly known as "real life."

■　　■　　■

There is one other thing. If you watch *Star Trek*, look for yourself.

You will be there.

Part One

THE BEGINNING

· · ·

There is a sense in which time is always present as space. Quantum physicists and astronomers describe the time–space differential as the result of space travel at (or near) the speed of light. And yet the point at which space becomes time (and the reverse) exists as a constant in everyday life as the verb *to be*.

"Where *are* you?" carries within it the unspoken word *now*.

"What time *is* it?" implies both *now* and *here, in this space*.

Among the many unanswerable questions I have pondered over the years was one posed by my son when he was about six years old. When asked "What time is it?" he replied, "What time is *what*?"

This is the very heart of the spiraled and unending quest in *Star Trek*: "What does it mean *to be*? In this time, in this space, who are we?" Its struggle to answer those questions is a tale of time slippage and alternate space, a delicate and determined unraveling of current quantum theory—physics to metaphysics and back again.

Quantum theory gives rise to the postulation that the

universe consists of several linear, simultaneously active dimensions that coexist as interweaving patterns of time-space that are not relative to one another except at "weak points" where they meet. It indicates that several worlds may cohabit the same space at the same time and remain unperceived because the "fabric" of one dimension is atomically dissimilar to the pattern of another. Only at random points of exceedingly low probability could the nontime–nonspace between these dimensions ever be traversed. *Star Trek*'s quest was to somehow leap over that chasm called "between"—to discover the random, the serendipitous, the luminous light shining through the tightly woven cloth of our timespace reality, to break through, as it were, and leave our swaddling clothes behind.

Gene Roddenberry once told me that he "did not believe in time." Perhaps he didn't. He never spoke of the future in the future tense, to me. It was always "The future is," not "The future will be." He said he saw it—that it was present, within him. Perhaps it was this claim, more than any other, that prompted fans to dub Gene Roddenberry a "visionary," a title that was attached to him so often and for so long that it became a credential: Gene Roddenberry, Visionary.

Be that as it may, the absolute conviction that there *is* a future is largely responsible for the stunning impact *Star Trek* has had on American culture. *Star Trek* is a household name, not merely because it is entertaining enough to engage the capricious attention of the viewing public, but because it speaks to the fundamental longing of the human race to *be*— to survive, and *to survive happily* into the future.

Gene Roddenberry's favorite description of humanity was *a child race*. He seemed to believe that in the great cosmic scale of evolution, we were in the sandbox. Sometimes he changed that description to *an adolescent species*; other times, he equated our level of development to that of ten-year-olds. Whatever the metaphor, *Star Trek* writers have always built into each script the notion that to reach maturity as a species we must rely on something bred in our bones: goodness. It is that simple, and that complex. Perhaps the very reason for its magnetism is the fact that *Star Trek* has a message we have all heard before and believed and tried, until it got too hard or didn't work or didn't appear clever enough to others. Until we grew up just a little too far past a luminous infancy, and not far enough into the sagacity of experience. *Star Trek* reaches into the kindergartens and kitchen tables of our minds and says, "To survive, you must be good. There is such a thing as goodness. It is the hallmark of the human race. Believe in it."

Star Trek confirms human impulses and early teaching—it preserves a certain naïveté. It replaces the confidence and loyalty we once as a nation gave to our leaders, when once, we actually believed they were Kirks and Picards. *Star Trek* insists that if men and women of conscience sit at a round table, there will be knights, both male and female—there will be Camelot. *Star Trek* looks at the founding of nations, governments, and cultures of the future, the way our forefathers did, with liberty and justice for all. It is a very old-fashioned television show, about an incredible future that depends on the ability to keep learning from mistakes, to say that even if the United States of America does not work the way it was meant to, the United Federation of Planets will—or that it will work better. *Star Trek* upholds Jeffersonian principles.

It also holds sacred a natural property of childhood: daydreams, insisting that if you believe in fairies, Tinkerbell will live. Or rather, if you believe in other life-forms, you will look for them, build space stations and spaceships, and find ways to explore the galaxy. If you find them, you will have each made a wondrous discovery in each other. If you don't, you will find yourself part of a spacefaring culture, with a whole universe of possibilities to discover and a whole history of whatever it took to get you there—and that in itself will point the way to further discovery. Either way, you will win. You will be on a journey.

Gene maintained that the underlying message was intentional—that he had insisted it be incorporated into the body of *Star Trek* work. From what perspective he arrived at that conclusion, it is difficult to determine. Certainly various writers, producers, executives, and other people involved with the series have different stories. In the years since Gene died, I have heard or read most of them.

But in 1991, I had not yet heard these points of view, and in any case my mandate was *to record what Gene had to say*, true or not. I believed most of what he told me at the time. I had no reason not to. But, actually, I don't think it matters much—the medium in this case is the message, and whether Gene practiced what he preached, lied, exaggerated, was self-deluded, or whether he was a paragon of virtue really has little to do with the fact that he said what he said. After all, it makes little difference if "Thou shalt not kill" is recommended by a saint or a murderer—it's still a good maxim to follow. What I do not like, in retrospect, is the fact that he did not give credit where credit was due for creative ideas—never once mentioned Matt Jefferies, who designed the sets, the props, the very core of *Star Trek*—the *Enterprise*. Nor did he mention a good many other people without whom there simply would have been no *Star Trek* at all. But then I didn't ask him those kinds of questions, although it would have been fitting for him to offer such information in his answers. I simply asked him who he was, what he thought—and why.

Sometimes, Gene would say that he was just a guy—that what he *now* thought was the product of many years of thinking. At other times, he would hint at a more metaphysical reason for his views, touch on something that he refused to explain. Most of the time, he would simply say, "I don't know," a phrase he said was the beginning of the answer to everything, the first commandment in his particular branch of ontology. He did say, consistently, that he had an obligation to find answers.

Millions felt that he did. When Gene, by some self-engendered quantum leap, entered the outer reaches of a future dimension he called *Star Trek*—and found it wondrous—he (and Herbert F. Solow, then head of Desilu Studios) gathered the best—writers, directors, creative and support staff—to bring that wonder into focus for the people who would watch it. Gene Roddenberry, with the help of that brilliant team, created a television show of the same name, not to depict the details of that future, but to demonstrate what it would take to get there.

In its vision of the future, *Star Trek* pushed the principles of equality a little further forward. In *Star Trek*, equality is kinetic, quick, and real. It is not equal opportunity, but equal reality. It means that everyone's stomach *is* full, not potentially full, and that everyone's home is a decent place to live. It has a lot to do with the verb *to be*. Or as Gene remarked in several of his speeches, "We are on a journey to keep an appointment with *whatever we are*."

Equality means, in *Star Trek*, that there is no equal pay for equal work—there is no pay for any work, because one works for the love of it and no other reason. Everyone's real job, according to *Star Trek*, is to explore what it means to be human; to refuse to accept what we perceive as the limits of the human mind, to ignore them; to traverse every possible dimension of outer space and find out what's out there; and to travel every possible level of intradimensional mind space and find out what's in there.

In *Star Trek*, the greatest praise is the word *human* and the greatest condemnation is interference—to violate the inner space of anyone else, to not leave him alone to dream his dreams, to live her life. Inherent to this philosophy is the

Prime Directive, the principle of noninterference on which the world of *Star Trek* depends. In that maxim, the shows challenge the philosophical dialectic between help and hindrance, between personal ethics and cosmic morality. The greatest challenge—in all four nonanimation incarnations of *Star Trek*—is to determine how the inviolate aloneness of each human person can interface not only with other humans, but machines and other life-forms when—and only when—the human race takes its final leap into maturity.

Roddenberry and a stunning group of talent built a bridge to tomorrow with the materials of today: curiosity, tolerance, openness, intelligence, discipline, daydreams, a willingness to help, technology, love, determination, and courage. All those things exist within us, *Star Trek* says. Use them.

Gene's job, he so often said, was to daydream—and to return from the world of dreams to the life he led as "just a guy" and explain it to others.

Among many extraordinary things about Gene Roddenberry were certain habits of childhood kept, by design or innocence, within him, and yet he never remained a boy. He was very definitely a man—an adult of the species he was wont to call "child." Sometimes it seemed he was of some other species altogether. Although in poor health during our interviews and declining daily, he was a powerfully present man, a contradictory measure of wisdom and stubbornness—a paradoxical and amorphous mixture of freedom and constraint.

Old, ill, reflective, Roddenberry appeared to be a contemplative agnostic. His favorite discussion with me was how to form a peaceful, fluid, interconnective system of peaceful coexistence while retaining a forceful self-identity; or put more simply, how to meaningfully share who we are with others and still remain intact.

He made a lot of mistakes, he said, and took pleasure in pointing them out as milestones of achievement. To recognize mistakes, he stated, was the greatest progress anyone could make.

Gene and I shared very little in terms of experience. He was exactly my father's age. Having been born near Pearl Harbor just after a war in which Gene flew eighty-nine missions as a U.S. Army Air Corps pilot in the Pacific, I am certain that my existence on this planet is directly connected to the results of those and hundreds of similar missions. My childhood was filled with stories of men like him—men who at the time the stories were being told were busy trying to forget what had engendered them. But not Gene. He said he "needed to understand everything." He would exhibit such tenderness for the human race that when I asked questions such as "How does that relate to your having killed so many of them?" he would plunge into a quest for an answer as if his own life depended on it.

We shared almost nothing of personality. His personality fluctuated according to circumstance, for reasons which he addresses in this book. His character remained the same. We met in the last few months of his life, and yet we spent more time talking together about the things that mattered most to him than he had done with many others whom he had known for years. He insisted on it. He brought me home to his house, to his family, so that I would have no chance to mistake him for a television producer or any other image that public life necessarily imposes. In some ways, this was a disadvantage. I cannot now, nor have I ever been able to, see him from the outside in.

Our conversations were secluded and confined, the product of the last few months of a man's life. What he said, what he did, what I saw, in that very circumscribed time and space is all I can offer.

Gene said more than once that we were of the same species, he and I—with a penchant for camouflage, a horror of intrusion, a fascination with inner and outer space, and a certain relativity factor in which nothing was constant except that which we meant when we said "I." Of course, that kind of statement can as easily be false as true: no one likes to be transparent; no one likes what s/he deems to be interference; everyone is fascinated with the human condition, internal and sociological; and most people have a core of self-identity. I assumed then that he meant by these words what I would have meant if I said them—and I questioned them no further.

In fact, no two people could be more unalike than Gene Roddenberry and I. What we shared was the human condition that everyone shares, as well as an interest in why its depiction in the guise of *Star Trek* had become such a success. Perhaps a more specific commonality was belief in a personal dreamworld, the preservation of which superseded any necessity to dispense facts. If there is one truth I can state unequivocally, it is that I saw a far more private version of the man than any of his interviews, public speaking, and surface activities revealed. There is little in this book that can be gleaned from any other source.

We talked until he could no longer speak and communicated for much longer than that. He made requests of me on his deathbed, told me his most well kept secret, entrusted to my care what he said he loved most. He called me "changeling"; I called him "Sister Mary Gene." We both knew who was who. I don't know why he first agreed to do this book, before he knew me. He said once that it was the letter I wrote him. Another time, he insisted that the book was his own idea.

When he became aware inside that he was dying, his revelations became more urgent. The closer he grew to his final hour, the more he told me—sometimes in a word, sometimes one short sentence at a time. "Write about Majel," he said once when I had thought he was sleeping. "Explain about Hitler," he said another time, giving me permission to write about something I was wondering whether to include or not. "Go to the studio. . . . Find Bob Justman . . . tell Leonard . . . Spock . . . Majel. . . ."

And then he was gone.

Some months later, I went to some of those whom he called intimate friends, men he had told me understood something inside him that others did not. Of those, I interviewed only a few, not as a matter of an arbitrary selection process, but because I quickly realized that it was a mistake. This book was intended to be the result of primary contact, and, as it began that way, I felt it should continue that way. It was also a mistake for another reason. The group of men he called intimates were part of a generation that, as one of them told me, "toughs it out." Some of the questions I had to ask were not the kind that would allow the pain of his death to stay decently beneath the surface, and so, with great respect, courtesy, kindness, and a sincere wish to help, they did not answer them. They would say, to a man, as if he had not died, "Well, that's something Gene has to answer."

In the end, I decided to incorporate very little secondary information. This is not that kind of book. It is a book about the beginning of self-revelation, cut short by death.

These were the last interviews he gave, the last extended conversations he had. They represent his latest thinking, and what is equally important, according to his own equation, his latest feeling. Do they define him? No. Nothing does. They do paint a portrait of something about him, something that reached out and touched millions of people, every day. But they do not represent all that he was, in part because they do not represent all that he said.

Majel once said, "He tells everybody what he thinks they want to hear." I'm sure she was right, except that people don't usually have the energy for such duplicity when they are dying. I think there was some genuine frankness—if not of fact, then of feeling, in these last few weeks of his life. And where there was not, there are two choices for the reader: (1) ignore the inaccuracies—the material still makes for interesting reading; (2) read *Inside Star Trek* by Herbert F. Solow and Robert H. Justman—there, you will find both truth and fact.

On second thought, do both. The comparison is fascinating.

Part Two

THE MIDDLE

. . .

Worlds shrink as they expand, I remember thinking, walking across the lot at Paramount Pictures on my way to first contact, as it is called in *Star Trek* terminology, with Gene Roddenberry. *First contact* refers to the initial encounter of the *Enterprise* crew with an alien species. A portentous event in any relationship, first contact is the fork in the road, the turning point, the open gate. From the televisions of the nation and the world, where *Star Trek* has been seen in one form or another for over twenty-five years, to the University of California Press's idea to do a series examining the components of the American genius, the phenomenon of *Star Trek* was creeping back slowly to its womb, its embryonic origins, its primal cell. It was all contracting, like "a star pulled together by gravity,"[2] into the one intense point of creation—the mind of Gene Roddenberry.

I was early, an alien in a now-familiar world. It seemed

---

[2]A phrase coined by Gene's friend, Robert Jastrow, in *Red Giants and White Dwarfs.*

somehow appropriate as I approached the Hart Building that there were two skies at Paramount: the real one, brown and hazy, and the bright pristine "on a clear day you can see forever" one, standing on the lot like a giant drive-in movie, to make life on screen look real, or maybe to look as unreal as our perception of it.

We met before we met, in the manner of children—curious, apprehensive, and eager—for when I peered around the edge of the door that separated us, leaning to the left just enough to catch a glimpse of the man before we were introduced, there he was, leaning to the right, peeking around the door frame just enough to catch a glimpse of me. In a kind of salute, we raised our hands and smiled, unstartled and, it seemed, mutually relieved. Someone introduced us, or didn't.

My poster of Einstein was on his wall. The sun was shining—or wasn't. We looked at each other appraisingly for a long time. This was our first conversation:

Me: "You're not shy, are you? You look shy."

Gene: "I think I can be."

Me: "Oh dear."

Gene: "Are you?"

Me: "No."

Gene: "Okay. I won't be either."

■　　■　　■

The second time we meet, he says, "You haven't asked me one fact about myself."

"Do you want me to?" I ask.

"No. Not at all. Let's just talk—as we are."

I begin to launch into another subject.

"But why haven't you?" he interrupts.

I start to remind him that this isn't a biography, but he knows that. He wants the real answer.

"I don't think you are facts," I say. He looks at me with a

pleased, surprised wonder. "There is a passage in *The Little Prince* that I read as a child," I tell him. "It made sense then. It continues to make sense." I quote the paragraph as accurately as I can:

Grown-ups love figures. When you tell them you have made a new friend, they never ask you any questions about essential matters. They never say to you, "What does his voice sound like? What games does he love best? Does he collect butterflies?" Instead, they demand: "How old is he? Does he have any brothers? How much does he weigh? How much money does his father make?" Only from these figures do they think they have learned anything about him.

Delight spreads across his face. "I think I am going to love telling you things," he says.

■   ■   ■

His voice sounded like tomorrow.
The game he loved best was being.
He collected ideas.

■   ■   ■

He sits back with some satisfaction. "Now," he says, "let's see if we can figure out who this Gene Roddenberry is."

"Okay. What is the difference between truth and integrity?" I ask.

"Truth and integrity . . ." he muses. "Boy, you really cut through the crap, don't you?"

"I try. I was impressed by something I read that you said about relative truth. I think your fourth-grade teacher accused you of something you didn't do—and you defended yourself up to a point, and then just said, what the hell—yeah, I did it."

"Yes," he says with a laugh.

"Well, some people will stand and fight forever and consider themselves people of integrity for having done so—whereas you basically told a lie. If you know something to be true and it is true, and you try to explain it to someone who is not ready for it or doesn't want to hear it, do you undo yourself as a vehicle for true communication if you insist on facts as truth? Is that it? Are you offering a false image of yourself to insist on the truth—in these circumstances, I mean?"

"Oh yes—and there's so much of that. There are certain things you know to be true, the revealment of which is just not worth it—for all the losses you take. You have to be true to yourself. Let's explore that later—because that's typical of what I have done."

"Okay. What is the relationship between power and creativity?"

"Well, certainly they are related. I have a power in *Star Trek* that allows me to express my creativity that I didn't have before. I think that relationship has something to do with the power of a free mind—a kind of freedom you feel inside yourself. I don't create if I don't *feel* my own power to do so. But really—I don't have a feeling of powerlessness; generally, I do have a feeling of power."

"Do you know where it comes from?"

"I like to believe that it comes from the rich mix of things that—" he begins, then stops abruptly. He looks at me hesitantly. We do not know each other well enough yet. "No. I don't. But it's there. I've never doubted that my power was there—but I've had reason to doubt that I could force the world into marching the way I wanted it to march."

Until *Star Trek*? I wonder but don't ask. I am assuming it will become clear.

"Who never fails you?"

"There's no person that has never failed me—any more than I am capable of not failing anybody. Humanity never fails me. They never fail me. But people? Oh yes."

"They?"

"Well, yes. I'm not speaking of my humanity, you see, but humans—all humans. Not individuals, but the whole human race. I think that humans are incredible—they are the most fascinating things in the universe."

"Well, but, Gene, you haven't been through the whole universe. It may be that 'there are more things in heaven and earth, Horatio . . .'"

"Oh yes, there very well may be—that's what I try to show on *Star Trek*."

"I want you to talk about that later. But first, tell me what the difference is between people and humanity."

"I have a theory about that. I call it a socio-organism. You see, the usual way of the physical world is to progress toward unity. When life originated on this planet, it was a single-cell organism—and perhaps by accident, or a need for survival, or some primal urge, these individual cells began to group together to form collectives, then units, then a corporate body. And that's what happens on a larger scale with humans. They form groups—tribes, nations, and so on. Even a simple working unit, like a business or a factory, is a socio-organism, because the individual units—or people—come together for a single purpose. Right now, in most cases at least, the purpose of collectives in society is functionary— to produce a product or to band together for economic or defense reasons. But if you follow the thought logically, you can project a more complex interaction—perhaps a thinking body in which the individual units no longer function in any capacity as individuals. They may specialize, but not without the knowledge and cooperation of the whole group. It's a kind of interdependence in which the whole is greater than the sum of its parts. I think this will form a new species—a human collective. I think we may be headed that way. It seems to me a natural consequence of evolution."

"Like the Gaia principle?"

"Yes, very much like that."

"Which means that it could be a step backward, if, as some scientists point out, we began that way."

"I don't think it is, though. It may be a recurring cycle, but it is a spiral. Each time we come around again, we will have learned something from our previous forms of unity. We may develop our capacity to . . . to think to each other, for example to a higher level, each time we take another step in the evolutionary chain."

"Thinking to each other exists now—on a rudimentary level. You know people, don't you, that you would describe as being on the same wavelength—to whom you can give a quick glance to impart a thought?"

"Yes, I do. And I try to do that with as many people as I can. It rarely works," he says rather wistfully, then brightens. "But sometimes I am fortunate in that attempt. What I'm speaking of is large groups of people who have a group consciousness on a regular basis."

"Sounds like a convent or monastery to me."

"How would you know that?"

"Because I was in one—many years ago."

"What? You mean a convent school?"

"No. I mean a convent. You know, nuns, silence, uniformity, interdependence. Socio-organism."

He is dumbfounded. "You were a nun?"

"Yes. Don't worry; it's not contagious. But it is a socio-organism. We got to the point where, living together day in and day out, largely in silence, that other forms of communi-

cation developed. It was fascinating. We could almost think
to each other."

"When?"

"When what?"

"When were you a . . . ?"

"Nun. It's not a bad word. '66 to '69. Same time as *Star
Trek*. And, you know, that was one of the few programs that
we were allowed to watch!"

He stares at me.

"It was a long time ago. A lot has happened since then. My
point is that it was a perfect example of your socio-organism
idea."

He recovers. "Yes. Uh—how?"

"Mostly by regarding the face, rather than the dots. I was
reading a book by Paul Davies, called *God and the New
Physics*, in which he discusses reductionism and holism. And
he says that no amount of scrutinizing the dots on a newspa-
per picture can give you an adequate concept of what the face
looks like. Whereas in a convent—or at least the kind I was
in—the object is continually to form a face. Like on a
starship, I suppose. Is that why you study humanity instead of
people? To see its face? Why you look at the socio-organism
as being representative of the true nature of man (humankind), rather than individuals?"

"I suppose it is. That is why diversity is so important.
Because in diversity, you can trace certain properties of
the human spirit that transcend differences. It is only
when you look at what unites humans rather than what
divides them that you have some idea of what it means to be
human."

"That's another thing Davies points out—that you can't
always take a problem apart in order to solve it. Sometimes
you solve it only by putting it together. And so you think that
the human race is gradually moving toward an understanding of itself by creating a socio-organism?"

"I think that might be the case, although the argument for the individual is very strong. My socio-organism theory is that a certain individualism might remain but become more and more specialized, so that one unit is proficient in one area and another in another area. They are codependent, or really interdependent with all the others—so that the whole species becomes a true organism."

"Isn't that self-defeating?" I ask him. "Because who is left, then, to see the whole picture?"

"Yes, you have a point. It does tend to imply that the individual self, as we know it—as we conceive of selfhood—would be defeated. But that might not necessarily be a bad thing. Because maybe everyone sees the whole picture: there is a collective eye, so to speak."

"But how would we learn anything if we kept to our individual tasks? It sounds a bleak future—the antithesis of what your philosophy seems to offer."

"You did not feel it bleak in your convent, I'm guessing."

"No, not at all. But that was because the socio-organism of it was just that: socio-, or perhaps religio-. It wasn't a single-intellect organism. Each of us studied a variety of things—worked at an enormous number of tasks."

"Well, I haven't worked it out yet," he says comfortably, as though he were contemplating no more than his next move in a chess game. "What may function today as an organism or prototype organism may be very different from what we see tomorrow. And maybe there will be the opportunity for both individuals and cells in the great cosmic wheel. It just seems to me that it already exists—is somehow intrinsic to the need of humans to merge—and the impossibility of that being satisfied by individual mergings and couplings, such as marriages or fragmented political or national entities or religions. I feel that we are on the path to a collective that I can't quite visualize."

"But maybe you're looking at a metaphysical thing physically."

"What do you mean?" Gene asks. "I don't think I am."

"Well, let's consider you as the primal cell—your mind as an analogy of the first single-celled organism. That mind produces an idea like *Star Trek*, and within months, the idea is transplanted into thousands—millions—of minds as a modus operandi. These millions continue to do what they do, but in a way that speaks of and to the primal cell. Physically, socially distinct, but mentally, philosophically connected."

"Yes, for now," he says slowly, with an uncertain emphasis on *now* as though he is not quite sure what the word means. "But what happens as a result of that idea transplant is what I'm trying to see. This is just a stage; people want to do things with these ideas—and they will. And that draws them into contact with each other. And they build the kind of world in which perhaps a certain kind of diversity becomes extinct. That's what I worry about."

"Why?" I argue. "Diversity for its own sake isn't particularly helpful. It's one thing to celebrate it because it exists. It's another thing to mourn its passing if it no longer works. That's like saying people shouldn't marry those of other races because we have to preserve racial purity—that we have to stay distinct, diverse. The opposite of taking delight in diversity isn't to condemn it; it's just to allow it to change naturally. We may become diverse in ways we don't know about yet."

"Yes, that is true," he replies, "but that isn't what we can concentrate on—now. That's an idea for the future, when diversity has been celebrated and accepted. You're leaping ahead. And I suppose I am too, with my socio-organism idea. We mustn't do that. Humans are a fearful species. And I have certain fears about that too. But I have written a great deal about this, and I can give you my ideas on paper. Then we can discuss its moral implications.[3] I'd like to do that." He pauses and looks at me speculatively. "A nun, huh?"

"Yeah."

He shakes his head.

■   ■   ■

In a 1985 letter to Dr. Charles Musès, Gene wrote:

Assuming the socio-organisms do continue to evolve more and more control of their human cells, successive generations of children will have less and less ability to act as individuals. Some interesting questions in this. Will the sorgs (socio-organisms) eventually win and destroy human individualism? Or is it possible the human creature is dividing (as some species in the past have done) and become two human types, individuals and sorg? No less interesting is the question of whether there are not pleasures and comfort in being a sorg cell that amply repay what is lost in giving up individualism? I don't know and maybe can't know because I'm so prejudiced in favor of individualism. . . . Agree that there is nothing intrinsically ethical about the size of human organizations per se, but somehow the citizens of the large developing nations with advanced education and media and medicine and technology do seem more civilized and peaceful than those of agricultural and preindustrial nations. Could this suggest that the evolving of individual and sorg cells may be the pathway by which the cosmos's intelligent individual life forms into even more intelligent superorganisms? It pains me even to suspect this could be true—that is, it pains me until I

---

[3]After Gene died, Majel and I went through boxes and boxes of his papers. The socio-organism paper was among many items that were discovered to be missing in the days following Gene's death.

require myself to think of it as an uncommitted intelligence (or scientist) might think of it.

■   ■   ■

In *Star Trek: The Next Generation*, there is a race of half-humanoid, half-machine creatures called the Borg. The parallel with the sorg is striking, and yet the cybernetic Borg present a serious threat to the Federation. The original concept for the Borg was an insect race, and traces of that idea remain. Their collective mentality, homing instinct, and singleness of purpose are strongly reminiscent of the hive or the anthill. Certainly, they are not the independent, spirited explorers of space one would expect to encounter in a race as technologically advanced as they. The Borg seem to have no spirit. They are devoid of feeling, devoid even of thinking. It is characteristic of the diversity of the *Star Trek* universe to include a rock creature who is a tender mother (the Horta, "Devil in the Dark," *Star Trek*, the original series) and a group of altered humanoids (Borg) who maintain their babies in filing cabinets ("Q Who," *Star Trek: The Next Generation*). In the years that preceded our discussion, Star Trek philosophy fluctuated between a fascination with collective consciousness and a fierce, parental protectionism for the independent individual of the human species. In keeping with a fine regard for the independence of the individual, it came down rather heavily in favor of individualism; hence, the sinister threat of the Borg race. Privately, Gene didn't think it mattered all that much, saying to me once that he had thought about it a great deal and that if there were some cosmic insistence on unification, it would take place as naturally and painlessly slowly as previous evolution, so that whatever life-form resulted would think it as preposterous to bemoan a previous state as we now would to complain that we were no longer individual units of single-celled protoplasmic entities, floating independently in a primordial swamp.[4]

.　　.　　.

Nothing stares us in the face as we take our places at the table. It is a menacing sight, nothing. With its cavernous hunger, without even the promise of a black hole, into which one might metaphysically fall and contract and become a dense world among worlds, it seeks us from across the table. The waiter brings bread. We are avoiding fear. "What do you most fear?" I had asked him, not ten minutes before, while the phones rang in his office and a secretary bobbed in and out on a wave of words like an errant buoy. "Let's get out of here," he had said. Walking to lunch, he answers the question. "Nothing," he says. And now, in the commissary at Paramount Pictures, Inc., we sit thoughtfully, crumbling bits of bread. Nothing grins maliciously. Self-revelation is near.

"Fear," Gene says, in a neutral tone. "I wonder what else you're going to ask me." I hand him my list of questions. He looks them over and decides to be recalcitrant. "I think your questions are a lot more intelligent than my answers are going to be. I don't know if I can answer them."

"I don't see that 'What do you most fear?' is a particularly brilliant question. Do you want to avoid this question?"

"Yes, I do," he says. "But, now that it's been asked, I don't think I can. It's sitting here between us. The uninvited guest."

"Oh, we invited him," I say. A waiter comes to take our order. He is deferential in his serving of egos and appetites.

---

[4]Gene did not write the episode "Q Who." The connection is mine. And yet, somehow, this illustrates the philosophy of Star Trek, for out of the thousands of scripts that *could* have been made into episodes, few were chosen. What is engendered from an original seed is a population of ideas, each of which forms a cell in the philosophical organism. (Obviously the choice of script depends on its excellence, suitability, cost, etc. I am speaking here of choices made within those economic and practical parameters.)

Little things begin to appear on the table—unasked for, and yet more welcome than the unanswered question between us. Lemons and sugar, ice cubes and wine, cream, extra cream, new flowers. Gene orders two salads and looks at me through narrowed eyes. He is not sure how I will take being ordered for. "It's a good salad," he says as though in challenge. "It's the best."

I thank him. Someone stops at the table. Gene introduces me. "This is my mistress," he says pleasantly. He lets the joke stand for a few minutes, waiting to see if I will correct it. I outwait him. He reintroduces me properly, and we chat for a few minutes. I see the possibility of discussing nothing fade. When a second person drops by the table, Gene introduces him to me as his lover. Nothing disappears.

■ ■ ■

Humor as defense, I think as I fly back to the Bay Area that afternoon with the question still unanswered. At 11 P.M., the telephone rings. "This is Gene Roddenberry," a now-familiar voice announces. "I would like to answer that question." I get my notebook, which proves to be unnecessary. The answer is "Humanity."

I write in my notebook, anyway, what he says next. "I have a great fear that our human leaders will fail to understand that a world such as *Star Trek* is possible—that all the glorious things—not that *Star Trek* represents, but that the human being represents—will fall on deaf ears. That frightens me. There's always a chance that not enough humans will understand and appreciate themselves enough to make a great change in the human equation."

It sounds like a prepared statement—unmistakably sincere, deeply motivated, but prepared all the same. I thank him for answering the question. He asks when I can come down next, reminds me that I will be staying at his house. We make a tentative arrangement. Just before we hang up, he asks, "What are you afraid of?"

I say I will write it down and give it to him when I get there. "Oh, good," he says. "I wrote mine down."

■　　■　　■

Fear follows us into his office one peculiarly clear morning. He wants to hear what I have written.
I read it aloud:

I am afraid that evil will win out over good. I am afraid that there is no real wonder left in the world—which is why we as a species frantically try to create it—hence, Hollywood. I am afraid that I won't learn what I am supposed to learn before I die and that it will somehow be my fault for not having tried hard enough. I am afraid that I will never touch the true human condition, because I've been too happy and too fulfilled, and that consequently, I am less human than I should be. I'm afraid of madness—not mine, but the fact that it exists—that so much can go wrong with the human brain. I'm not afraid to make the mistakes we all make (although I don't like to, of course), but rather, I am afraid that I might make the larger cosmic mistakes of missed destiny and dimensions unperceived. I'm afraid that I won't be able to do enough in my allotted span. And I am afraid of surrender—not human connection, not intimacy, but surrender. Afraid of the power I have, because it is so difficult to translate into action accurately. I am afraid of pain for my children. I'm not personally afraid of emotional pain—I don't seem to be vulnerable to that on the deepest level, but even that raises the question about whether that's a good thing. It may mean that I am not human enough. Afraid that the great cosmic truth, whatever it is, may be beyond my capacity to understand, if ever the time comes for me to understand it, and therefore, I will be disqualified from vowing allegiance to it.

"Read it again," is all he says when I have finished. I do. I add that I do not necessarily believe these things—such as the fact that there may be no wonder in the world. I believe there is. But when worries do arise, they wear the garments of these concerns.

"I could have written that," he says. "Most of it. In fact, I'm not sure I didn't, somewhere in my mind." He frowns. "So—we share certain fears . . . who would have thought it?"

"Don't you want to add anything? Delete anything?"

"No. Nor do I want to discuss anything. Let it stand for the purposes of this book. It's enough for folks to think about without getting into detail."

He looks at me keenly. We have suddenly leapt light-years closer to each other.

"What about nothing?" I ask him.

"Nothing?"

"You know—when I asked you last week what you were afraid of and you said 'Nothing.' Was it a literal answer? Are you afraid of there being nothing out there, in the universe—that we may discover nothing? No creator? No cosmic consciousness? Nothingness?"

"I don't know. What would you say if I asked you the same question?" he replies, making circles on his finger with his thumb.

"I would say no. No, that's one thing I am definitely not afraid of."

"May I share that answer with you, until one of us knows for certain?"

"You don't want to discuss it."

"No."

■ ■ ■

He is afraid of that, of course. His particular tendency being the examination of all possibilities, he won't have missed that one. But being afraid of a possibility does not mean that one believes the possibility is probable. Or the reverse. He just doesn't want to talk about it.

Yet.

. . .

I write a note to myself during this conversation. It says, "'The Changeling,' original series—*Star Trek: The Motion Picture.*" There are a few, later scribbles in the margin, added as an afterthought. One is a question from the Baltimore Catechism: "Who made you—and why?" They all refer to the search for one's creator.

In one of Gene's films, *The Questor Tapes*, the protagonist, Questor, is an android seeking his maker. His human friend, Jim, accompanies him on a journey halfway around the world to find the scientist who created him. At one point, when the search seems futile, Jim says to Questor, "Suppose he isn't a good man? Suppose he isn't even sane?" To which the android replies, "One's creator not sane? An interesting question. How would you answer that in your own case, my friend?"

. . .

"The human race thus finds itself unique in the dubious distinction of being the first biological species able—if it continues on certain psychological collision courses—to become insane. Fortunately, the diagnosis also indicates the remedy," wrote Dr. Charles Musès, in *Destiny and Control in Human Systems*, to which his old, dear friend, Gene Roddenberry, suggested that he add Christopher Fry's "A Sleep of Prisoners" to intimate the remedy:

> The frozen misery
> Of centuries breaks, cracks, begins to move;
> The thunder is the thunder of the floes.

THE MIDDLE

The thaw, the flood, the upstart spring,
Thank God our time is now, when wrong
Comes up to face us everywhere,
Never to leave us til we take
The longest stride of soul men ever took.

I ask Dr. Musès one dark December afternoon why Gene chose that particular poem for him. "It was a favorite of his," the great scholar replies. "It expresses his true religion—a far cry from atheism."

There is something dark and Decemberish in both of these minds: both see illusion and reality exchanging places in an evolution to which they feel similarly responsible to bring some kind of light. There is, in fact, illumination between them. Gene Roddenberry called Charles Musès his mentor— refers to him now as a most intimate friend. He is the one person, Gene says, "who understood *Star Trek* long before I or anyone else . . ." There are secrets between them.

■   ■   ■

"What moves you?" I am prompted to ask, one day, watching the wind lift his hair. We are on our way to another lunch at the commissary. "Not moves as motivation, but what touches you—affects you?"

"I would say it has to be the same answer—humanity."

I begin to feel that my book will consist of one word. "Gene," I say, "you're going to be terribly devastated if we do go out into space and find other life-forms who are more fascinating than we are."

"Not 'if'—when. Space is humanity's future. And I don't know that that is necessarily true; they may be equally fascinating, not more."

"You don't think that there is a possibility that we may discover something more interesting than ourselves?"

"Oh, there's a good *possibility*," he says affably, in the

reserved way that one mother acknowledges the beauty of another's baby. "But I haven't found it."

"Are you looking?"

"So far, I have found nothing that says that humans are not supremely fascinating—supremely successful in the broad definition of what *successful* is. I can't find a single thing about humanity that sounds a false note."

■　　■　　■

What moved him? I can absolutely answer that for Gene. People. Humanity moved Gene.

—*Robert H. Justman*

He was his own common denominator—as obsessive about humanity as though from some cosmic coupling, he had spawned the whole human race. Every answer to every question, when reduced to its final sum—its primal end and beginning were nothing less than all that we are: alpha, omega, and all in between. Humanity moved him, seduced him, terrified him, calmed, soothed, overjoyed, and perplexed him. It weighed him down, buoyed him up, inspired and eluded him. In this preoccupation, he resembled nothing so much as Q.[5]

---

[5]Part of a corporate mind/entity/race called the Q Continuum, Q is one manifestation of his species. He is a being or state of being (or beings) that we never quite comprehend. The Q (and Q, brilliantly portrayed by John DeLancie) are among the most fascinating aliens of the *Star Trek* universe. Q is so often infuriating—and so often right. He is the nemesis of the *Enterprise*, charming, insincere, manipulative, callous. We dislike him (most of the time), we fear him (some of the time), we are angered—even outraged—by him (nearly all of the time), and yet, despite ourselves, we look forward to Q's arrival because we learn a little more about ourselves from him. From the first episode, "Encounter at Farpoint," through various escapades and incidents, he continues to baffle, annoy, endanger, confound, and enrage us, and yet his antics are curiously ineffectual. In the end, despite all he can do, we remain standing. Q never really defeats us, because he somehow seems to need us—or perhaps because he never really understand us. Our humanity is our defense.

When I ask him if he has a Q streak, he laughs and says yes. "Out of the mouth of Q come some very important Gene Roddenberry questions," he says. "We need to look at ourselves, examine who we are and why we are taking this fork in the road and not that one. Q has little or no compassion for the human race he loves to taunt, but that doesn't matter. It is the questions that matter, and how the human race will answer some of these questions for itself that ultimately will matter."

Q's preoccupation and interference with the human race engenders questions of being: What does it mean to be human? What does it mean to be, in fact, since we are mortal and Q is not? Is it morally correct to think that saving one human life is worth risking hundreds of others? Are we an incorporate species, or a loose collection of individual units whose very separateness absolves one of responsibility toward another or many others? Are the needs of the many greater than the needs of the few—or the one?

"What kinds of questions?" I ask Gene.

"Well, let me see—what is Q's challenge to the human race? To see the large picture, perhaps. To realize that there is a universe out there of which we are only a very small part. That we have more than a personal, a national, or even a global responsibility to evolve into a greater life-form than we are. To find a broader definition for the word *human* than we are currently comfortable with. And I think Q is there to show us the morality of power. You asked me about power and creativity. The correct use of power feeds creativity. And the misuse of power destroys it. Our people are very cautious of power in *Star Trek*, and rightly so. They are not ready for it. The human brain is still far too divided in its impulses to be reliable. But we are getting there. We are so much improved in the twenty-fourth century. That is the beauty of humanity. It continues to improve, despite its contradictory impulses of creativity and destruction."

■　　■　　■

The next time he brings up a great love for humanity, I ask him how he reconciles that with having killed people. He starts to talk about a new series he has created in his mind, which he will never make, about a society of subtle and rational Hitlers. It is so terrifying that it answers the question, but he goes on to say about World War II that "those things seemed necessary, and I seemed to be drawn into them by necessity—perhaps by some ignorance."

I ask him how a twenty-fourth-century guy fights a twentieth-century war and comes through unbroken. Suddenly, the air around us changes. Gene Roddenberry recedes swiftly into a tunnel of time from which he is normally free. He looks at me with my father's eyes, from somewhere I have never been. I have seen that look a thousand times in my lifetime, from a generation of men I will never see again. "Don't ask," it says. "Stay ignorant. Stay innocent. Be the daughters, wives, mothers we left behind. Don't see what I am seeing. And please, don't understand." He shakes his head unconsciously and I know that even now, almost fifty years after the war, he will not answer my question. He will give an answer, but not the one he would give to another soldier—another guy. He returns from memory to philosophy, and sighs.

"I'm not unbroken," he says, finally. "I'm patched up. And it isn't because of a reason you might think of. It's not because of the violence and horror of war itself, although that was terrible, really terrible. It's because it wasn't just some kind of mistake—it wasn't an aberration of man's nature—it *was* man's nature. It was because I came up against the manifestation of what had been only a fantasy for me: the existence, the persistence, of evil. And something inside me broke when I found out that you can't fight evil with good— at least not always. You might be able to prevent it from erupting by being assiduously good, by making good choices. If enough people in a society make that choice. But after

40

you've let it rise—and the people of Germany let it rise, and
the world let it rise—you have to confront it with itself. You
have to be what it is, in order to overcome it. You have to
confront yourself."

"The enemy within?"[6]

"Exactly. That's what it means to know your enemy. And
that's the real reason that we are both good and evil inside.
So we recognize it in others—in movements and governments and so on. So we can survive."

    ■   ■   ■

"The Enemy Within," a *Star Trek* Original Series first-
season episode, is a classic study of good and evil within
oneself. When a transporter malfunction causes Captain Kirk
to be beamed aboard the *Enterprise* in duplicate, one intelligent and compassionate, the other amoral and dominated by
primal urges, we see one of *Star Trek*'s most fundamental
concerns: the synthesis between the animal brain and the
forebrain, which Gene believed was essential to the evolution
of the human race. Most significant in this episode is the
attribution of "good" characteristics inherent in the "bad"
persona of Kirk, and the reverse.

    ■   ■   ■

"You mean two wrongs do make a right, after all?" I
remark.

"Yes, sometimes they do. Two wrong actions—not two
wrong motivations. If it was wrong for the Nazis to kill, it was
just as wrong for us to kill. But it makes a difference what the
reason is. And we have to live with that and hope that

---

[6]The ability to dissect morality, to examine by implication and logic the
fundamentals of right and wrong at the point of origin and/or coexistence, was
one of Gene's preoccupations at the time I knew him, and one with which he
unceasingly turned to Hitler as a study of the human organism.

whatever good comes out of it far, far outweighs the bad. And on the scale of human history, diplomacy is a recent invention. What we may once have fought over, we may now negotiate peaceably. But there is always so much ignorance and emotion to combat."

> I do not object to violence itself, on television. I have a son growing up. There are some types of violence I would prefer for him to see. I don't want him to see dishonest violence. I want him to see that if a grown man hits another man in the face with his fist, that knuckles break and bones shatter, and that is a messy, harmful, stupid thing to do. . . . If I had not been in a censored medium, the violence I would have shown on *Star Trek* at times would have been much more real. . . . We have had 35 years of war movies in this country, and usually the hero clutches his breast and dies very quietly, sometimes with a little smile on his face for having been able to give his all. I think during those 35 years, if our soldiers had died in pictorial depiction in movies and in television the way those of us who have been in combat know that men die, often screaming their guts out, we would have had a lot less people saying, yeah, let's send our kids to war.

> —*Congressional Statement of Gene Roddenberry*

■   ■   ■

For some reason, this reminds him of his days on the Los Angeles police force.

"About my being a policeman for a while . . . I never had any doubt that one of the great problems of modern times was how to force people to obey the law. It seemed to me at one time in my life that the best way to do that was to have policemen that were justifiable—policemen that were very good, policemen who lived by what we consider the law. I think I would have done a better job than Chief Gates has done. At one time it was considered by some people that my natural future was to become chief of police."

"I'm glad you didn't."

He laughs. "I don't know . . ."

"Well, there wouldn't have been any *Star Trek*."

"There wouldn't have been any *Star Trek*, but there would have been a much better police department."

"A Starfleet on Earth?"

"I think I could have. And I had the courage to try new things. At one time, I had decided that when I became chief of police, or when I graduated from being a police sergeant to police chief, I would bring along with me new attitudes and new uniforms—and that the only weapon you carried was one with which you could *choose* to injure or kill someone . . . or not. I felt there should have been shades of weaponry."

"Like phasers?"

"Like phasers."

"There is a kind of phaser out now."

"Yeah—tasers. And my thinking was innovative in many areas. I knew exactly the answer to the drug question. I had written—researched and written—a piece for Chief Parker that pointed out that drugs created a no-win situation for the police. Unlike some police chiefs, I believed that we should legalize drugs—with penalties, with certain costs to their use, but in a way that it doesn't make a criminal out of you. I suspected that the answer to drugs did not lay in making them illegal. I would have done something like I have done in *Star Trek* for law enforcement. It might have failed, but that's the way I would have had it. I think it would have been a brave and bold try."

"Because people wouldn't be developing these highly toxic, instantly addictive drugs if they had access to other drugs, like in Switzerland? No reason to make cheaperstreet-value substances that do quick, irreparable . . . damage?"

"Yes. And you wouldn't have had the underworld running America as they do today."

I remark that the biggest cocaine bust in California to date was made a few days earlier in the affluent northern California community in which I live—just a few blocks from my house. His answer disturbs me: "This just confirms that the laws that relate to drugs are foolish."

"Are they?" I ask.

"Of course."

"Well, I don't think they're going to change."

"Oh, they'll change," says Gene, "when various people take a civilized view of drugs and the danger of drugs, or the so-called danger of drugs. I don't think that drugs are terribly dangerous. I think they are dangerous in the same way that it is dangerous to eat too much, or . . ." He fades off for a moment and then begins again. "I have never been one who thought that there was a great effect of drugs on people. The effect of drugs on people is so intertwined with the effect of happiness and pleasure on people. People who are pinched and so on and hate for people to have any joy; they're the ones who create the problems with drugs."

This seems to me to be so patently stupid that I make no reply. I have worked in correctional centers for children and teens and in hospitals that treat babies born with drug dependencies. This ends up, therefore, not being a conversation, and I omit it from the original manuscript.

■　　■　　■

He tells me a little more about his Hitler series. It is a far less visible and less obvious erosion of fundamental precepts than history recounts. There is no suspicion, no opposition. Everything seems good. No one wakes up suddenly in horror, because everyone has given up the right to think and therefore the ability to distinguish right from wrong. "We are creatures of *emotion*," he says, "and what this said to humanity, during the time of Adolf Hitler, was that Hitler offered some things that we had relaxed our *thinking* about—and it would have gone Hitler's way, if he had been a rational man. I think that if Hitler had played his cards wiser and better—and portrayed essentially the same person that he did—but with more care about what his real motives were, he would have won."

"You mean you think that people wanted what he had to offer?"

"Enough that he could have gotten by with it, yes—as long as he hid his true motives. People were passionately stupid about this need for a national emotion. To feel passionate about organization and order. To feel emotional about *things*." Gene snorts.

"Well, he was an irrational man. Irrationality often masquerades as high feeling."

"Thank God. Because if he had been a rational bad guy, he would have turned the world upside down. Oh, yes—plenty of people wanted what he wanted: trains that run on time and all the things that make life simpler. We were lucky in his irrationalism. And therein lies a beautiful series."

He looks at me piercingly. "Just think," he says, "what would have happened if Hitler had been *good*."

"Arthur C. Clarke wrote a novel," I say, "called *Childhood's End*, which has some of that feeling."

"Oh, yes—but the opposite happens in *Childhood's End*. The devils turn out to be decent guys."

"But the attitude of the people was similar. It looked like it could be a Hitler situation."

"Yes, it did. It was great, wasn't it?" he asks, glancing at the row of Heinleins, Asimovs, and Clarkes on his bookshelves.

"Yes. Compelling. But here's something I want to ask you. What difference would it have made, philosophically, if

Hitler had been good, if he espoused the same premise, which I suppose was that he knew best and would think, act, and operate on behalf of everyone? And used the same fervent oratory? You still end up with an unthinking populace. Or does goodness not permit autocracy?"

"Those are some of the questions that I am exploring in this series."

"Got any answers?"

"One: that good can be evil and evil can be good, depending on circumstances. And that's a very good question you asked about—well, about ends and means. Of course, the atrocities that went on wouldn't have happened—and that is good. But as to your question about an unthinking populace, well, this is something that frightens me, as I told you. And yet, there are so many out there that don't know how to think, and *think* that they think, well, I don't know. People need leaders. And I think it is absolutely imperative that they be good, decent people. But as to whether they should, in their goodness, allow others less qualified to participate in decisions that they are incapable of making, no; that isn't goodness, it's disaster. I wouldn't let anyone do that in my show. And I hope I'm basically a good man. But I know my show. I decide. You see, you get someone writing a marvelous script, for example—really first class. And they have a thousand extras in it and hundreds of thousands in special effects. And it's filmed in Tokyo. And they keep saying, 'But it's a good script, it's a good script.' Yes. It is, but I can't use it, because I know what it takes to make a television show. Or they have Picard getting drunk and shooting someone—in a story that would be excellent for another show, a way of demonstrating a heroic flaw. But it's not *Star Trek*. It's not Picard. He wouldn't do that. This is the twenty-fourth century and Picard is Picard—with his own flaws, which I created. And of course I won't use it because it's not *Star Trek*. And this kind of power that I have is not because I'm smarter—no. In fact, put that same writer in my office for a couple of days, and he'd smarten up astronomically. My power comes as the creator—and because *I know my work.* And that's a rather silly example of the kinds of decisions I make in my work. And I expect from our leaders in government, science, medicine, commerce the same kind of knowing. I think we must insist on a kind of excellence of mind, of experience, and if that experience means age, then age, in our leaders. I think we have to look for something that cannot be measured or analyzed, but it can be recognized, and that is the quality of leadership itself: the ability to feel and think in balance, the ability to engender emotion for rational aims. Really, I sometimes wonder if it wouldn't be wise to have an emotional president and a rational one. Equally in power."

■   ■   ■

On October 13, 1992, a little more than a year after this conversation, a *San Francisco Chronicle* column by Jon Carroll appears called "We Really Need a New King Thing."

The American President is both head of the state and the head of government and that just ain't right. . . . The British have a Prime Minister and a Queen. . . . [Of course we can't have a king] because we fought an entire war so that America would never be ruled by a king. So not a king, but a king thing. We need a name for the job, that's the first step. *We need a name that commands respect the world around* [italics added], and yet is free from old associations and connotations. Not proconsul, duke or chief. Not mogul, sultan or CEO. Not satrap or secretary or emperor. We need a name that is at once familiar and new. The new job should be called *Captain-kirk* [italics added].

47

This person, he goes on to say, should have "physical stamina, natural dignity, and an established place in the culture" and that "the President and the Captainkirk would rule jointly. . . ."

It really isn't a serious article. But it could be. I wish Gene could have seen it.

■   ■   ■

"I think there are some who simply must be told what to do, by compassionate leaders," Gene continues, in this same conversation. "But told respectfully. You see, Captain Kirk is a good man. And he is also an excellent man—well trained, experienced. But he is a man who was *born* to be a leader. And whatever that is, it is what makes him capable of convincing others who are less experienced, less able, to allow him to lead. In his leadership, he gives others the opportunity to grow. He isn't so in love with leading that he forgets his duty. His duty is to seek out life—and that also means the lives in his care—to bring them along, to see that they have the opportunity to learn and grow to their fullest—their fullest may not be a quarter of what Kirk's is, but it's theirs and they have a right to it."

"Are we talking about Kirk or Gene or Hitler or the president of the United States?"

"All leaders. That's why I have this series in my mind about leadership and power. It's a series that I'll never make, though. I don't think I want to get into another gigantic series."

"It does sound daunting. But then, you never get tired of *Star Trek.*"

"No, but if I wanted to fit my brain for this new series, I could find many reasons that I would like to show the Hitlers in this way—so there would be weeks passing by without any sign that they were fucking the world. And we would see how people would respond to that—the conflict of emotion and freedom, the need to feel part of something, and the coldness of rational freedom. But I'll never make it. I just don't feel like it right now."

"What do you feel like, right now?"

"Writing, I think. I have so many ideas in mind. Most of them are books; some may survive the translation into television or film. I don't know. Right now, at the moment, I like being here with you, talking about the things that matter to me. Because they don't matter just to me, you see; they matter to everyone, even if they don't know it. It is a terrible mistake to think that the future is somewhere off in a distant time. It is here—in embryo. We are creating it right now, with the decisions we make about the environment, with the attitude we take toward space exploration, with the education we are giving our children. Everything." He sighs and shrugs his shoulders, like Atlas shifting the earth to a more comfortable position. "But . . . talk to me for a little while. Tell me what comes into your mind because of what I have said."

"Oh, a lot of things: most of all, the way we think, the way we struggle with our thoughts and never let them free. Just freeing a thought sometimes makes enormous changes. I think that is what makes *Star Trek* what it is—neither an appeal to the emotions nor an argument for cold rationalism. It's both, and therefore neither. And that gives credence to prescience—to all the inventions and attitudes, all the thoughts and habits and cultures, diversity we encounter in *Star Trek*. It brings time into perspective. It changes the meaning of tomorrow. When you say *education*, it's not just a word that means a passport to a linear series of events in an individual's life. It means the education of the species."

"Oh," he says animatedly, "I've given so many lectures on that very concept. And people are so frightened of it, they never comment on it. They pretend they didn't hear that part of the lecture, or if they mention it, they say, 'Yeah, neat—great idea.' But they are terrified."

"Terrified about what?"

"The giving up of cherished concepts, things they think they need to be able to recognize themselves as human beings."

"Like what?"

"Like anything. Think of something fundamental to your beliefs that you wouldn't be willing to give up."

"Give up in favor of what?"

"Well, now," he says, raising both hands in a kind of universal appeal, "you see, that's a question that most people just don't get around to asking. They think of something dear to them and panic—won't go any farther in their thoughts."

"Oh—well, that doesn't make any sense to me. Thoughts are the only province of pure being left to us. Besides, you don't have to do anything about what you think. You can just think it. And anyway, I do have some experience in at least the metaphysical sacrificial aspects of life: I gave up just about everything when I went into the convent."

"Except your beliefs."

"Oh, no, no—not at all. I had no beliefs when I went in that I wasn't willing to give up; and I had no beliefs when I came out that I wasn't willing to give up, for a good reason. Don't mistake Catholicism for a religion. It isn't. It's a nationality, as someone once said. Belief has very little to do with it."

"How could it not?" Gene asks. He seems to be having a very good time asking questions. We will have an argument later about this very fact. He will win, which is why this conversation appears at all.

"It really isn't necessary to believe like a Catholic," I tell him. "It's only necessary to think like one. Because, in the end, after all that study and training and a lot of things that you can't possibly know—and I'm not going to tell you right now—what I found out was that the only requisite belief—

for those who explore it deeply enough—is the supremacy of 'an informed conscience.' That's what they tell you in the end, and what the Jesuits sometimes—and the Benedictines usually—hint at in theology classes, like you hint around at things in *Star Trek* and hope that people will recognize. The rest of the stuff is for the people who don't. And what that means is self-governance—'mortifying the passions' and all that—for those who choose it. And blind obedience for those who don't. Like *Star Trek*."

He looks very surprised, and very interested. "Like *Star Trek*. Hmmm. Well, but what does it mean to think like a Catholic?"

"Gene, I am supposed to be interviewing you."

"Well, it is *I* who wants to know."

I shrug. "Okay." I figure that I can just eliminate this conversation when it is time to put the book together. "Well, briefly, it means a habit of rational analysis, no matter how irrational the premise, a constant awareness of culpability, an internal detachment from all but primary exigency. It means a large vocabulary at a very young age, which includes words and phrases like *transubstantiation* and the difference between *actual grace* and *sanctifying grace* and—oh, Gene, it's a whole culture. It means being able to explain those things to the satisfaction of a series of philosophically exacting instructors. It means a grounding in Latin that results in making English words mean to oneself something other than their colloquial use would generally imply. It means carrying around a world of images—and thinking in metaphors— living in a metaphorical world. Nothing is really literal, after you've finished the two thousand questions or so in the Baltimore Catechism at age seven. It all seems to apply to everything except the dogma, which one soon learns is another metaphor—made literal for the lazy or the inept. Or at least that's the way it was—and I suppose, remains for many people my age. I don't know; I haven't been involved in that in years. The point is, it's just another *Star Trek*, if you separate the content from the form, and deal with—well—with what *is*."

I can see his mind buzzing, but we are not yet quite known to each other. He is being careful. He says only, "Oh, but I wonder if most people separate things like you and I. I don't think so somehow—it's something I am still trying to find out. I think, so far, that they are afraid of detachment. Of being detached from what they perceive as themselves. Which is why I think my socio-organism idea would work. And anyway, I may have been a little cruel in my insistence on the giving up of cherished ideas. I don't remember. I just remember that I scared quite a few people."

．　　．　　．

Unclouded vision ahead requires that you deal with what is. To deal with what is, you must free your forebrain of your personal value system and personal preferences. You must discard all—or at least most—of your prejudices. Not just simple intolerance about race, religion, and so on. It is much more difficult than that. You must free your mind of those values dearest of all to you: affection for your home, your background, your country, its customs, your own culture, your religious beliefs. The more precious the belief to you, the more certainly it must go if you are to free your forebrain to use its perception and logic. Some very able and intelligent people are unable to endure this exercise, even for a few hours. Some people get angry at even the suggestion that they drop all their preferences. Almost a castration complex—"I can't give that up!" At a recent conference, someone asked, "Why go to all that trouble? Why not just read some good books about the future?" Which falls into the category of questions you wish that pleasant, intelligent-looking people didn't ask. Aside from the not

inconsiderable advantages of learning to free your forebrain to do what it is clearly designed to do, I shudder at
the thought of anyone making a trip as important and
perilous as tomorrow while totally depending on someone else's vision.

—*Gene Roddenberry, university lecture*

"Well, anyway, tell me: give up in favor of what?"

"I certainly don't need to answer that question for you.
And I'm not going to answer it, personally, for publication.
I'll tell you later. But perhaps I will say this for publication: in
favor of not letting the concerns of our animal brain override
the impulses of our forebrain. To somehow distinguish between intelligence and instinct."

■   ■   ■

We now know that each of us has an early brain
combination that we can call our "animal brain," which
supplies our unthinking needs such as heartbeat, re-
flexes, and other body operations necessary to life. It also
provides us with our emotions, fear, anger, hunger, lust,
family protection—all the drives we've needed in order
to survive and to reproduce. This animal brain is rela-
tively small and simple compared to the wondrous thing
that rises out atop it. Wow! If you want to feel awed and
humble at whatever created us, you need only consider
our magnificent forebrain, the cerebrum. That forebrain,
too seldom described, even to us who own them, is a
mini-micro-miniaturized wonder that makes our finest
computers look like simple baby blocks.

Let me now cup that forebrain within my palms
here—and I invite those who want to share a very
unusual feeling to do the same. Try it. You might like the
feeling. Incidentally, despite whatever you might have
heard, all of us have almost identical-size brains. Ready?

We are holding within our palms now ten billion electrical signal–producing neuron cells . . . with each of those ten billion neuron cells able to interact in different patterns with as many as twenty thousand other neuron cells. Which means . . . that this "natural computer" small enough to fit within our palms is capable of three hundred trillion interconnections, which gives this young and frail human creature's mind an options potential equal to the total number of stars in our galaxy! . . . Our magnificent forebrain does all those things that make us "human." It gives us our ability to think consciously, to love, to write poetry and great symphonies, to theorize about relativity, to study quasars millions of light-years away, and at the same time, look deep inside the construction of the atom and of our gene cells too. It also gives us reason with which to regulate our smaller, sometimes too selfish but very necessary animal brain.

Our "animal within us" brain is lovely in its way too. Its insistent, basic message—survive! reproduce!—is not the "evil" part of us unless nature and life are evil things. In fact, the animal brain is capable of simple and marvelous delights, that part of ourselves which propels us into dance and into song and into sacrificing of our families. Why can't we control that simpler brain? Well, the fact is that we do control it! Billions of humans succeed in doing that every day. Very ordinary people like us have controlled it even in the face of torture and death. Dare we learn more about how to control it? *Dare we not learn that?* There is something patently obscene about a three-hundred-trillion-options magnificence being held hostage by a small, simpler, half-tamed animal thing.

—*Gene Roddenberry, university lecture*

■　　■　　■

54

"What about the reverse?" I ask him. "Allowing instinct to take over sometimes? I mean, the ability to do something—the intelligence needed to create a nuclear weapon, for example—is at variance with the instinct to survive, and logic dictates some sort of 'discard mechanism'—an idea Dumpster—in the animal brain that would rule in favor of survival."

"Oh. That is an interesting way of looking at it—backwards, yes, but I think that recognizing the implications of an intelligent act, such as creating the bomb, would also rest with the forebrain. The forebrain then informs the animal brain that it is dangerous, and then instinct takes over."

"So the object may be to create a third mechanism—the synthesis brain—that does not think sequentially but operates outside time and sees all ramifications at once."

"That's called wisdom," he says, "and some humans already have it, but unfortunately, not the ones who should—not the ones with the power."

"You have quite a lot of power. Do you feel it an obligation to be wise?"

"I feel an obligation to try. I like that concept of spontaneous synthesis. That's what we have in computers today. And coupled with the human brain, we have the future, not only in our hands, but quite literally, in our minds."

"Speaking of coupling with the human brain, you had a concept once that was never developed on *Star Trek*. In your book, *Star Trek: The Motion Picture,* you had Kirk receiving a message from Starfleet via a computer implant—a 'senceiver' in his skull. Why didn't you use that device in the next series?"

"I don't know. I think I thought of it, but it doesn't work for television—how does the audience get the message? It would be confusing and annoying to be doing constant voiceovers in that fashion. It's a good idea, but some things don't work for television. We'd have to invent a gesture—like tapping one's head or something—and then it would just look silly. That's what I'm thinking now; I don't know that I thought it then. But if it could work, it might be a thing we could try. I certainly like the idea—and I think it likely that some sort of technology like that will be in place then."

"Yes, and they wouldn't be vulnerable to having their communicator badges stolen, et cetera. You did something similar in 'Patterns of Force' in the original series, but it was a simple locating device and didn't appear again."

"Well, I'd love it. I think we are getting closer to the time in which computers will be part of our internal structure, as we have false joints and pacemakers and other wonderful things that enhance human life now. Computers are as close to an answer about the future as we'll ever have right now."

"Why *Star Trek*, Gene?" I ask him. "Why not *Cowboy Trek* or *Deep Sea Trek*?"

"When you say, 'Why *Star Trek*? Why not *Deep Sea Trek*,' that misses the whole point of what I was trying to do. I was trying to affect everyone in the audience. *Deep Sea Trek* would not. That would have been limited. But I wanted to basically get something that commented on the future and said something about the future, and the others would have been too limited. Once we pick space for it to be about, we make it much broader than the other subjects you mentioned. It is not an accident that our spaceships opened up the idea of the computers. Once you have chosen space, you're stuck with the fact that there will be so much information generated to undertake these journeys that computers would have to become more and more sophisticated. And it was fun for me too, because suddenly I found that people were asking me questions—a guy who was, a few years before, a cop, and suddenly, I was the expert. I had to invent a warp speed that would take us outside of this—"

"*You* did that?"

"Oh yes," he says happily. "It was obvious from the first that we needed warp speed, because if we traveled just ordinary subwarp speeds, the television show would be running years before you could get anywhere."

"Yes. Plus, your relative age to everybody else would be—well, you could never go back to Starfleet, for example, because everybody would be dead and there would be a whole new crew," I respond. "Going out into deep space, your relative age to everyone on Earth would change."

"Yeah, but we did stay away from the age thing. It's true that when you get into space travel at various speeds and so on that you would have—well, we just ignored the whole problem of age because it is so complex! To think that you could have your grandchildren and great-grandchildren and present children all be operating in the same arena of space because of the various warp speeds."

"Madeleine L'Engle in *A Wrinkle in Time* explains time as a taut string on which we walk from one end to the other. But if you make the string loose, then bring the two ends together, you can move from point A to point B in one step. Like this." I take the cord of the tape recorder and demonstrate.

Gene looks instantly intent. "It *is* something like that!"

He adds, "But we could not overcomplicate warp speed—because there are various warp speeds—and we had to keep the factors consistent. I had to say there will be different warp speeds because we need them to get to very, very different planets, and then that's the only way we could be believable. . . ."

"Well, Asimov does the same thing, but he solved the problem by inventing the 'jump' to hyperspace, which I understand to be the elimination of time. It is a different dimension. So when you get back to Earth, you're the same basic age—in the same time frame. It doesn't sound implausible, and anyway, mathematically, it's possible—or so they say."

"But the principal reason I refused to deal with it is that it would just make the television show too complex," Gene says, returning to producer mode.

"When I laid out our first design for the bridge, in the first series, I had only a general idea of what should be there. I knew that the quickest way to generate information was to have buttons that you pushed that would somehow connect to all that information in the computer. And without knowing what they were, what they meant, I just knew that they should be there. There was nowhere in those days where you could go to get a computer keyboard. We had to make ours out of wood! We *predated* the computer generation. That's why the computer industry was so helpful to us—back in the days when they were just solving certain mysteries, we were presenting and solving mysteries too. This is why they have been so supportive over the years. We kept having the experience of going to a top-rated computer company and having the boss say, 'Give them whatever they want!' It was grand to have them say, 'Take the shop—you *Star Trek* people obviously know more about it than we do!' We received hundreds of thousands of dollars' worth of information and help. And from NASA too."

"I have a question," I say, wondering if I should ask it.

He smiles. "You always do—and always ask it. There isn't anything that you can't ask me."

"Okay. It's about androids, which are the most sophisticated example of future computer technology currently under serious discussion—and the human brain. Would you like to be an android?"

"You have a reason for asking that question that I would like to hear before I answer it."

"Why? So you can tailor your answer? I don't want you to do that."

"No—so I can answer the question you are really asking. I'm not sure what it is."

"On *Star Trek*," I say, looking at him skeptically, "there are so many instances of mind transference, of telepathy, of entities cohabiting the same body, and of mechanical or computer interaction with humans, or humanoids. The 'Lights of Zetar' creatures; the androids in 'I, Mudd'; Roger Korby in 'What Are Little Girls Made Of?'; Kolos, in 'Is There in Truth No Beauty?'; Landru; Sargon; the Controller, in 'Spock's Brain'—and probably a lot more that I can't remember offhand. The Vulcan mind-meld has properties of mental intercommunication between beings, although generally it appears to be one way: Spock reading the other person's thoughts, not the other way around. But it's the android thing that puzzles me."

"Yes, we did do a lot of shows like that," he says noncommittally. "What's on your mind?"

"In every instance that I've mentioned, except the mind-meld, those connections are portrayed as undesirable. Perhaps less so in 'Is There in Truth No Beauty?,' but even so, it is a threat. But there is something about it that doesn't quite . . . ring true."

"What makes you say that?"

"I don't know—intuition, I guess. That, and also, those examples are all from the first series. When we get to the first movie—ten, twelve years later—you have Commander Decker disintegrating into a universe of molecules so that he can merge with V-Ger, which is basically a computer, even though you call it a 'living machine.' And this giving up of purely human life is portrayed with great excitement and anticipation—with exhilaration and celebration.'"[7]

---

[7]The desire to merge, to unify, to become one with another being, has always been a part of the passionate human existence. More than just an ensurance of the continuance of the species, our deepest connections reach beyond the mere physical, into the depths of the mind, psyche, and spirit. Union—in myriad forms and for myriad reasons—is not merely a recurring theme in *Star Trek*: it is a raison d'être. Gene Roddenberry was fascinated with the variety and depth of attraction and connection between humans and other beings and the endless

"Yes."

"Then comes *Star Trek: The Next Generation,* and there are Trills, Bynars, Borgs, and even Data, who, although purely android, engenders some of the same questions about life—or 'livingness.' "[8]

"I think I know what you're going to ask. Why did I treat those two concepts so differently, between the Original Series and *The Next Generation?*"

"Not quite. My question is, in fact, did you? It seemed to me that in 'I, Mudd,' for instance, when Uhura says she would like to have her brain implanted in an android body, to give up a purely human existence, you cut and go to commercial, and the audience is supposed to be horrified by that—by her desertion of her allegiance to flesh and blood during those two minutes or so, until the next segment resumes."

"Well, the audience is supposed to be persuaded to buy

---

number of ways in which one being can bond with another, each one of which can be called "love." Transcending race, gender, creed, appearance, and ideology, *Star Trek* purports that love in all forms is something to be celebrated, not feared. In this scene, the merging of a man and machine is spellbinding. V-Ger's mechanical probe, Ilia, and the human Commander Decker begin the spectacular journey into oneness that will create a new life-form.

[8]Bynars appear in a *Star Trek: The Next Generation* episode entitled "1001001." The Bynars are a benevolent race, so integrated with computers on their planet that they operate in pairs and speak a binary language. The Trills are symbiont beings, composed of a humanoid host body and a highly intelligent sluglike creature that lives in the torso of the host. Because of the longevity of the parasite creature, it may inhabit several different hosts during its life span. In the episode "The Host," we first meet this race. Dr. Beverly Crusher falls in love with a Trill who is fatally injured and whose parasitic component must be transferred temporarily to Commander Riker, a "brotherly" friend of Crusher's, while awaiting a new host en route. A number of fascinating questions arise as Beverly finds herself still in love with inner being, now in a man she regards as a brother. The question of who we are and what it is inside someone that we love is brought to a stunning conclusion when the new host arrives—*a woman.* The nature of love and sexuality is deeply explored in this provocative study of human emotion.

things from the sponsors in those two minutes, but I know what you mean."

"Yes—but I think *your* reason was to implant a moment of consideration of that possibility—a subliminal flash that it might just be something to think about. And then we come back, and it turns out that it was just a ruse: Uhura was stalling for time, and humanity triumphs once again. But does it? I mean, what is wrong with an android body equipped with a human brain? And isn't that an idea *you* stuck in *my* mind by doing that show? And isn't that an example of conveying a truth by telling a lie—because really, you're showing something to be bad, that you think might be good? In other words, is it better to present the idea—in whatever light—than not to present it at all? Or am I seeing things that aren't there?"

"Which question do you want me to answer?"

"All of them."

"Well, the simple answer is, I think, yes to everything except the last question. You're seeing things that are there. But I can't really give a simple answer, because I think that humanity is not ready to deal with the implications of all that would mean. Morality plays a large part in these considerations. I think that discussing the morality of this currently impossible technology for a century or so might bring us closer to the responsible use of this technology when it does become available. So, yes, I did intend that people think about these things. And no, I did not intend that they should now adopt the notion as a good one—only as a possible one, whose goodness or evil depended on its use."

■   ■   ■

Star Trek has always been a morality play. That's what it is about. That's what it's saying. You have all the premise you need to do a show like *Star Trek*—all you need to do is know the Ten Commandments. Morality is the subject that has intrigued humankind since the dawn of time—and will always continue to intrigue humans.

—Robert H. Justman

■   ■   ■

"And what about the first question?"

"What was that?"

"Would you like to be an android? Or rather to have your brain transferred to an android body?"

"Well, I haven't been very well lately, so that presents an attractive option for me. I'd certainly consider it. And, as you say, in *The Next Generation*, we are more comfortable with these things. Audiences have changed tremendously over the last twenty-five years. And, more importantly, for the show at least, I am as near to an absolute monarch as is possible in this industry. I have complete control over what my show says and does. Much, much more freedom. And far more direct responsibility for what goes out there to the audience. *I* am *Star Trek*. And as you say, we have wonderful options for interconnections between beings. I believe in those connections. I'm fascinated with the mind-meld, with the Bynars, with the Trills. To be able to understand another being—or beings—that intimately . . . oh, yes."

"Would you choose to be half of an entity? I can't imagine that you would."

"No. But I might like to let someone share me for a while, or I might like to share someone. But as a permanent condition, no. But others might. I don't create these shows entirely for myself. I seek out what humanity yearns for."

"What do you yearn for?"

"I said you could ask me anything. I didn't say that I would be able to provide an answer. If I knew, I would tell you, because whatever it was, I think you would understand it. But I just don't know. What do you yearn for?"

I tell him.

"Oh," he says. "Maybe that's it. But I don't think that's something I want to say right now."

"The preceding announcement was brought to you by the public Gene Roddenberry," I tell him.

He smiles. "I *am* a public figure." He looks into my face for a moment. "Don't worry," he says, "they'll figure it out."

.   .   .

Twenty-five months after his death, there will be an article in *Omni* magazine entitled "Souls in Silicon," by Frederik Pohl and Hans Moravec. Its subtitle is "Transferring the human brain to a computer may no longer be science fiction." "The future *is*," I hear Gene saying as I begin reading, "not the future *will be*."

.   .   .

We are having a particularly interesting breakfast. He is watching the news; I am reading a novel by Anita Brookner. We are both comfortable. That's the interesting part. When the news is over, he turns off the television and I put down my novel. We sit companionably for a few moments.

"I asked you once *who* never fails you," I say. "Now tell me *what* never fails you."

"My imagination never fails me. I don't leap spontaneously into an unfailing technique. I'm not that clever. I have to live with a thing in my mind for a considerable period of time—a character, for example. What never fails me is my optimism that in time I'll solve the problem that this thing poses. I can't promise myself that I'll do it rapidly, but sometimes I surprise myself. I have a rich mental life. That's why I had to make *Star Trek*. I felt I had something of importance to say, and if I could say it in a way that was entertaining to others, then maybe they would listen."

"What should they hear, when they listen?"

"Oh—so many many things. What comes to mind right now is space. Space is so important, because it affects our whole future. There is no doubt that we are going into space. *Star Trek* offers us the opportunity to choose big hunks of the future. How will we go into space? What is necessary? And I don't mean technology; I mean the development of the person—of all people. What kind of beings do we want to be? What can we give—and how will we make ourselves capable of giving ourselves to the experience of the future?"

■　　■　　■

Mankind will reach maturity on the day it learns to value diversity—of life and ideas. To be different is not necessarily to be ugly; to have a different idea is not necessarily to be wrong. The worst thing that could happen is for all of us to look and think and act alike. For if we cannot learn to value the small variations among our own kind here on Earth, then God help us when we get out into space and meet the variations that are almost certainly out there.

—*Gene Roddenberry*

■　　■　　■

64

Further conversation reveals that Gene believes it is the philosophy inherent in *Star Trek* that offers the opportunity to "choose big hunks of the future." It means thinking of space as one's natural environment, of Earth as one's temporary home, of country as one's school, and region as one's flavor. Family is everyone it can be, and love never means possession, greed, dependence, hobby, romance, sex, money, or revenge. Love in this world means *caritas*, an impersonal, impartial, universal regard for the sanctity of all life-forms. Above all, it means a passionate existence within oneself, a deep connection with the variety of beings that we each are inside. Its credo is Socratic: know thyself.

"To whom do *you* always listen?" I ask him. "Or almost always. Nobody listens to anybody all of the time."

"Really, no one. I have no such person—or group. I listen to the voice of . . . I listen to my inner logic."

"Where does it come from?"

"I don't know. It comes from—they come from—" He is changing his answer as he speaks. "This is a very weird thing. It's just an inner logic—an imagination that is right for me." Later he will contradict, expand, incorporate this statement into self-revelation. Later, when he is ready, he will tell me about Spock.[9]

"But many people have a friend or brother or someone whom they will always pay attention to when that other person speaks, because they trust their judgment on important issues."

---

[9]Spock is a half-breed member of the Vulcan race. Vulcans are humanoids whose ancestors were a passionate and violent people. At one point in their history, the consequences of these traits almost caused their extinction. In order to survive, they developed a philosophy of self-control, which was based on the suppression of emotion and the supremacy of logic. To admit to feeling emotion is the ultimate shame in their culture. Spock, however, is only half Vulcan. His

"I have no such person. So I guess the answer to that is: me!"

"Yes, I guess it is."

"You know that proposes—that sets—frightening goals for me, to know I know the answer. And I don't pretend that in every aspect of the world I do know the answer. But I don't know anyone who knows it better than I do."

"So—you are self-contained. At least you are if you consider your imagination to be you—or part of you."

"Yes, I am self-contained. But I'm not sure if my imagination is part of me—if anyone's is part of them."

"What would it be, if it wasn't?"

"A mystery. A flashlight in the dark. God."

"You're pretty well known for not believing in God. Do you claim him now?"

"Oh—well, people are often pretty well known for things that are not true."

"Well, is it?"

"No, it's not. I believe in a kind of god. It's just not other people's god. I reject religion. I accept the notion of God."

"But if you claim Him as personal imagination or source of

---

mother is a human, from Earth. And although Spock was given the same severe training as every other Vulcan child, it is as though he has twice the emotions and only half of the power to deal with them. He is in this sense a true alien, an alien even unto himself. This heritage has left him with a constant internal war. Only by sheer will and ceaseless effort is he able to function as a Vulcan. He is further impaired in his efforts by being the only Vulcan in a crew of predominantly Earth people whose warmth, humor, kindness, sorrows, feelings of all kinds, constantly threaten to undermine his fragile control. And because Vulcans are mildly telepathic by nature, he daily experiences a barrage of feelings that exhaust him. There is also the physiological cycle of pon farr, a kind of psychosexual heat that Vulcan males endure every seven years. The physical changes that this process initiates are fatal, unless they are "bonded" (mentally interlinked with a mate with whom they are also sexually active during this time).

imagination, then He—She, It—is not just a notion. You're begging the question, distancing it. 'The notion of God' is not the same thing as God."

"No, but they are equally abstract. I don't . . . humanify God."

"No. You just deify humanity."

He laughs. "Okay, look: whatever it is, we can't know it, but it very well may be there."

"Gene . . ."

"That answer doesn't satisfy you."

"Does it satisfy you?"

He frowns for a moment. "No—no, it doesn't. Let me think about it."

"I think you've thought about it. Perhaps you just don't want to reveal your thoughts. If so, just tell me."

"You're a hard person to dodge. And I don't want to dodge you—or the question. Yes, I have thought about it." He pauses. "All right. God, to me, is intrinsic to humanity. To the whole cause of humanity. To the imaginative principle. To what we create, and think. He—or I should say It—is a source, yes, but more an involvement with the unknown. God is like the leap outside oneself, something that has no discernible source, but is a source."

"Inspiration?"

"That's as good a word as any. Better than most."

"Well, the origin of the word is *inspiro*, from the Latin, meaning 'to breathe into.' Suggesting, in your definition, a breath of life from an unknown source."

"A breath of life. I like that. It is a breath of life—this God thing. It's not a thing you pray to, it's a thing you use to answer your own prayers. Humanity needs God in order to be humanity—it is part of them."

"Them. Not us."

"You've caught me again."

"Why *them*, Gene? Are you not human?"

"Yes . . ." He sounds hesitant. "Yes. Yes, of course I am . . . at least, my body is—this vessel is." He shakes his head dismissively.

"Well, we'll go back to that one. What I'm trying to ascertain is if you believe in a spiritual life."

"What do you mean exactly?"

"Do you believe that there is an existence beyond empiricism—beyond the body, beyond the mind?"

"I don't know that one exists."

"I know you don't *know*—nobody knows. *Credo quia absurdum.*"

"Translate, please."

"It means 'I believe *because* it *is* absurd.' In other words, one *believes* because one *can't* know. That is essentially the nature of belief, faith—in anything: the existence of aliens, the ability to overcome obstacles, some form of God. It's not about knowing, it's about believing—in oneself or anything else."

"Yes. I have faith in something that I can't know, but I don't know what that is. It's not the traditional Judeo-Christian God. It's that thing about humanity that makes them write poetry, paint great pictures. . . ."

"Create *Star Trek*."

"Oh—yes, that was a leap of faith. Creating *Star Trek* was a very spiritual experience, in that definition. . . . It really is a life beyond this one," he adds, flipping into metaphysics. "It's my world."

"Let's go back to 'them.' You can't seem to stop referring to humanity as though it were a separate species from yours. Why do you do that?"

"I don't know."

"Don't you?"

"No, no, I really don't. But I feel . . . apart, sometimes. Perhaps that's why I try so hard to connect to people. To humanity. I think many writers, poets, artists, stand apart. They are essentially creators, and creators, as someone said, have a spark of divine fire. Or, as you said, a breath of life. Perhaps it's that divinity in us that we call God—the creative principle. Answer the question yourself. Do you feel part of humanity?"

"This book isn't about me."

"But I'm interested."

"Oh, I'll tell you, but it's not going to form part of this book, so I'll just turn the recorder off."

"No—don't do that. I'm not here to pontificate. This is a dialogue—a dialectic. I find myself saying the things I say only because of what you say and ask. It's marvelous. It really is very liberating. That piece you wrote on the things that frighten us—that's the sort of thing that brings something into view that I wouldn't perhaps do on my own."

"We still haven't talked about it," I reply, thinking that it is perhaps the fear of there being no existence outside existence that makes it so difficult to address these questions.

"No, but we will. I'm thinking about it. And it's unlikely that I would be thinking about it right now without that—interchange."

"But, Gene . . ."

"No," he says stubbornly, "now don't try to dodge me. I want you to record this conversation."

"Gene, look—the purpose of this book is to portray who you are, not who I am. Nobody's going to care what I think."

"Then they would be very foolish. There is a wonderful thing created between two people when they communicate. Another being. Another entity. What arises between us is some kind of truth. And it arises only because you are you and I am me. If people want to know who I am, through this book, then they have to look at who you are. Because I choose it. Because you—you discover me. I might not even know what I really think in some instances, until a door that I had forgotten—or didn't even know was there—opens between us. That's the wonderful thing about a conversation—if it's a real one—if it's communication. It's like sex, which can result in a child. You have to have two parents if you want a child. This book between us is a child."

"Don't be silly. You could dictate your thoughts into a tape recorder."

"But they wouldn't be these thoughts. We're exploring Gene Roddenberry together—it's something that, at this stage of my life, is important to me. I want to continue to do that—as companions on an inner journey, as inner friends. I'm tired of interviews. This is a dialogue. It is creation. You can be—and are—that breath of life for me."

"Oh—so basically what you're saying is that I am God."

"Certainly. We both are. There is life here, isn't there?"

"Yes, but . . ."

"I can't reveal myself, for this purpose, without you. I really can't, you know. I'm not just saying that to be difficult. Besides, you can learn a lot about a person by the questions he asks of others. It shows what is in his own mind, what kind of quest he is on. I think what we're doing here is a marvelous example of what I'm trying to achieve—have always tried to achieve in *Star Trek*."

"Which is?"

"You tell me."

"To seek out new life—contact."

"Contact. Yes. Now please, answer my questions, and I'll answer yours," he says. "Do you feel that you are part of humanity?"

It seems a strange question to ask, even though I have just

asked it. But then, I do not refer to humanity as *they*. There is something hovering in his mind he can't quite reach. Nor can I. Suddenly old catechetical distinctions leap into my mind. *One is responsible for creating one's own soul.* "Yes," I reply, "whenever I'm not creating something else."

"You see? You see? That's exactly what I mean. You've just sparked something I want to talk about—the creative process."

"Good. Talk."

"Well, you've said, 'whenever I'm not creating something else.' It's that 'something else' that intrigues me. Because, you see, there really is a something else, as you know—as I know. I don't know what it is, but I go there—it's a place, really—when I want to create something. I—I think it's imagination, but that doesn't explain it fully. I feel very alone, you know. And I'm happy in that. I love myself. But when I go there—to this place of creativity, to this area of the mind—I know that's where I belong. What I find there, whether or not they are characters or ideas—whether or not they are the product of my own mind—are the species I belong to. What happens is that I bring them out into this world, the world of humanity, and they take their place among them." He gives me a quick smile. "Among us. But I don't think I create them. They already exist. I just—I just introduce them. That's really where the whole idea of *Star Trek* came from—from that place, or state of mind. And the creative process is not so much in determining what or who they are, or what they look like—it's figuring out how they will get to where we are. That's my job. That's my contribution. They will reveal themselves, who they are in our world. I'm just a vehicle—a transporter."

"So you reach into a sort of cosmic Oz and drag them back to Kansas."

"Yes. Although, sometimes, they come willingly."

"How?"

"I meditate—I think. I tune in, turn on, drop out, as Timothy Leary says. Or said. I don't think he is saying that nowadays."

"Tune in, turn on, drop out of what?"

"Myself, first of all. That's the tuning in. Or actually, the dropping out comes first. I just refuse to be part of this world for the time I am thinking. Then—then I tune into myself—I discover myself. And that turns me on, in two ways. Literally, I become excited about myself, my own mind. There's so much in there. And I turn on a kind of mental screening room. You know the screening rooms over at the studio—it's like that. I watch whatever is on the screen. I watch their faces, their movements. I see their backgrounds. I listen to their voices."

"Sort of a 'burning at the stake' activity."

"In another century, yes. Thank God humans have gotten beyond that stage." He thinks about this last statement, corrects himself. "*Are getting* beyond that stage."

"Why can't people get to Oz themselves? Or is that a question of Mohammed and the mountain?"

"Oh—well, people are afraid of that sort of thing. And I'm not a guru, dealing in states of nirvana, for others. It takes a great deal of energy, a great deal of longing, to get into that cosmic Oz, as you call it. I'm not sure everyone has the desire, or the ability."

"But you feel it is your mission to bring that longing to life—to bring back jewels from the Emerald City as evidence that it exists."

"Yes, I suppose I do. Only the jewels in this case are ideas."

I ask him why he feels such a desperate need to prove the existence of Oz.

"Because we need it," he says. "It may hold the answers to some of our most desperate questions. It is a world which can only be a world of ideas now, but may one day be the very reality we will live in. Ideas are life-giving. We need new life in order to evolve."

"New life and new civilizations?"

"I think so."

"Is this place a state of mind?" I ask him.

"Yes. Or a state of perception, I think might be a better way to describe it."

"Peopled with beings and objects that existed prior to your entering that state?"

"Yes."

"Give me an example."

He gives me an appraising look, makes a decision.

"Oh, that's the first easy question you've asked me. And an easy answer: Spock."

■   ■   ■

"I don't remember when I first met Spock," Gene says, sitting in the garden at Bellagio Road, watching Majel clip roses. "Although I know when I thought I created him. But now, it seems as if he were always there. I . . ." He stops, as if weighing the importance of his next words. "I love Spock," he says after a long pause, and squints into the sun. "I'm in love with Spock." The air is very still. He remains motionless, except for his eyes, which follow Majel's movements like a tracking device. The tape runs on, recording silence, punctuated by the occasional bark of a dog and the click of Majel's shoes on the paving stones. When she disappears into the house, laden with flowers, Gene turns. "Spock," he says. "Not Leonard."

"I know the difference."

He sighs. "Yes, well, I wish he did." His reverie seems to be melting, but before it is quite gone, he says something in a voice so low that I have to lean forward. When I hear what he says, I turn off the tape recorder, and we have an extraordinary conversation about his intense relationship with Leonard Nimoy.[10]

"Tell me about your relationship with Spock."

He brightens. "Oh—*that* is a relationship. It's very profound. Very powerful. In some ways, Spock is my best friend. I have long conversations with him. We're both trying to figure out the same problems."

"Which are?"

"The meaning of the universe. Who we are. Why we're here. The time and space of it all. Where we're going, and how we can prepare ourselves for the journey. You see, the journey takes place—is taking place—whether we are prepared or not. At least, that's what Spock says."

"Do you agree with him? Might we not stop our own journey, just by being unprepared, stupid, shortsighted?"

"Yes, I used to think that—that we could annihilate ourselves if we weren't careful. End of species. But now I tend to agree with him. The journey is inevitable. Humans will evolve; what they evolve into is their own responsibility. But the journey is unstoppable. We may end up in a nightmare of our own making, but it won't be in the same timespace we are in—or heading toward, now."

"You don't think we'll end up in a nightmare, do you? I mean, that seems inconsistent with your whole philosophy."

"Well, even I have lapses, but, no, you're right—I do not believe the future is anything but positive—because we've

---

[10]I write this only for the record, because what followed is something I promised to say only to Leonard Nimoy. I have said it. And in any case, it does not belong within the province of this book. Leonard Nimoy's enormous contribution to the creative evolution of Spock, always a sore point with Gene, is recognized and applauded by all others who were responsible for the show, including NBC. What is important here is Gene's insistence on the separation between his imaginary Spock and Leonard Nimoy's television character Spock.

already made that choice. I think technology will save us. And I think our own goodness will save us."

"What *is* goodness?"

"Basic human decency. An inborn resistance to inflicting pain on ourselves, on others. An ability to nurture our children, to protect them, is a good example of innate human goodness. Our ability to feel sorry, to sympathize with others. The wish to help. These things are part of our nature. The conflict comes when our needs conflict with those of others. And, of course, when we don't recognize what our needs really are. But we're learning. A century ago, the mentally disturbed were treated with the utmost cruelty and callousness. And now, at least we recognize the need to care for them, to find ways to treat or prevent such illnesses. Goodness is the impulse to improve the health and happiness of the species. I think that's clear. It becomes less clear between individuals, especially when one person regards another as responsible for his or her happiness. Then you have people saying, 'Oh, you are not good to me, because I want this or that and you will not give it to me.' That's bullshit. And there are a lot of conflicts about that. My meaning really refers to humanity as a whole. Individual conflicts don't really matter in that sense. It's the progress of the species that counts. Two neighbors may be at war with one another, but if we have just torn down the Berlin Wall, who cares?"

"Is goodness also not the avoidance of evil?"

"It is the avoidance, I think, of evil impulses in oneself, but, no—it is the confrontation with evil that is good, not the avoidance of it. But again, I'm speaking of humanity in general. People have to decide for themselves to avoid things, sometimes. Sometimes that's the only sensible thing to do."

"Do you forgive?"

"Oh, the questions you ask! Yes, I hope I can say that I forgive. I don't say that there will be no consequences of an act that may injure me, but I don't hold a grudge. I would be interested to know how you would answer that question."

"Oh, I don't know, Gene. There are so few things that really matter to me—I can count them on the fingers of one hand. Most injuries are petty annoyances. I just basically don't care—on the deepest level, I mean. On the surface, I might have a fit, but within a couple of days, or even a couple of hours, it doesn't matter. Most of what matters to me is so unperceivable anyway—by anyone except my family—and one or two old friends—that I am almost impossible to injure. It just doesn't apply."

Gene's face is a study.

"You look like you're trying to decide whether to say something or not," I remark.

"Yes, I am trying to decide. But as you've been honest enough to say it, I will too. And I hope that you will explain this, because I care so deeply—and yet, what you say is true. I don't care. I really don't." He looks surprised at himself and at me, then adds, "Well, not in that intense manner—about my own little unit of being. I think I fail to recognize the significance of injury sometimes. I have other things to care about. And, as you say, no one really knows what matters— or injures—Gene Roddenberry personally. And therefore, he is rarely really injured."

．　　．　　．

God is an entity in [the] process of growth . . . good and evil are only patterns which make experience and growth possible . . . no one ever really gets hurt because all of this that happens is happening only to that same great entity, and why worry about the "us" which is simply a fragment of that great consciousness?

—*Gene Roddenberry, letter to Dr. Charles Musès*

．　　．　　．

"And so—what does forgiveness mean?"

"Well, I suppose it means that we assume people have reasons for what they do, and so they do it. And if that somehow affects us adversely, we keep away from them. Or rather we keep them away from us. But we do not do them harm or wish them ill. And neither do we allow them to interfere with us again. Forgiveness is one thing. Stupidity is another." He looks at me curiously. "You must be very— free."

"Aren't you?"

"Yes. But I don't know many humans who are. You must be a changeling."

"And how does one recognize a changeling, except by being one oneself?"

"I told you." He laughs. "We are the same species."

"Speaking of changelings, you said that in some ways, Spock is your best friend. What about in other ways?"

"In other ways, he's me."

It makes sense, I think. An alter ego. But I am wrong about this, I discover later. "And when he's not you, who are you?"

"Oh, I'm Kirk. Captain Kirk."

·   ■   ·

Captain Kirk was Hamlet, the flawed hero. Gene told me that—early on. He modeled him on Captain Horatio Hornblower and he had characteristics of Hamlet, who knows what he has to do but agonizes over it, feels that, as Hornblower felt, that he had to put on a brave front for the sake of his crew, even though he felt that he really didn't have the requisite stuff, that he wasn't the sort of leader that he felt he ought to be. He wasn't strong enough, and yet he had to be strong, because otherwise they would have no one to protect them. . . . I think, looking back on it now, that Gene Roddenberry was Captain Kirk.

—*Robert H. Justman*

∎　　∎　　∎

"I remember reading somewhere," I remark, "not that it isn't obvious in the show, that you created Spock and Kirk as two halves of a whole. Would you still, upon reflection, say that that is true?"

"Oh, yes. Yes, it's definitely true. It is a profound relationship. A love relationship. Each has what the other needs in order to be a complete person. That relationship could be considered the essence of *Star Trek,* if you regard it as almost perfect contact between beings. I hesitate to say this for publication, because I don't want to be regarded as supporting the Kirk and Spock show. I don't. The other characters are very important. There is much more to *Star Trek* than Kirk and Spock. I'm just trying to indicate here that that relationship symbolizes on board the *Enterprise* what the mission of all of the characters is."

"Well, I can leave that statement out, if you like. Would you like me to?"

"No. Not if you include everything I've said. I want to make it clear that I'm not saying that *Star Trek* consists of Kirk and Spock; only that the depth of their relationship—their recognition of each other—is extraordinary, is something to be desired."

"Is that because both of them are you? Because if it is, you can't ask two people to have between them what one person has within himself."

"I think I can ask that of humanity," he says humbly and grandly at the same time. "I have such relationships with others. You do too. Perhaps because we're very similar. We may be in the early stages of such a beautiful friendship, but in twenty years' time, it won't be essentially any different; we may know more *about* each other, have had a few more experiences, but we will just confirm then what we know now. It has nothing to do with time. It has to do with capacity. And a kind of *chemistry* between people. You can't have that with everyone, but it's an ideal to work toward, reaching great depths and great heights. I've known people for ten, twenty years whom I am happy to call friend, but wouldn't dream of having a real conversation with. Not in this manner. And not that I wouldn't. But it takes both people—both have to have the desire, the attraction—and the capacity. *Star Trek's* message is really to increase capacity, to become more open and less fearful about these things. To become all that we are capable of becoming. To really touch others—become others— and not to be afraid that you will lose yourself—and to have fun with that, to enjoy it, without surrendering who you are. These kinds of love approximate—they are not identical to—the relationship you have with yourself, but they require the same abilities: to know oneself, to know others. *These are precious abilities we possess—and it's a terrible thing to waste them,*" he says fiercely as if I were poised to fly out the door the next minute and waste them. "And that is one of the reasons I say I am sometimes Spock, even though I would have to generally perceive myself as Kirk."

"You don't feel that you're a complete person, as just Gene/Kirk."

"Oh, no—no, not at all. I need Spock."

"Why?"

"Spock is, to me, the essence of evolution, in a sense, just as in another sense, of course, he's flawed. But he's a profound thinker—his logic is nearly perfect. He's not distracted, he doesn't excuse himself; he's very hard on himself, very disciplined. And he doesn't seek answers through emotion. He is undistractable, tenacious. He doesn't procrastinate; he sees a thing through, logically. He solves problems by refusing to allow himself to do anything other than focus on the problem."

"What if the problem is an emotional one?"

"Ah—you see, there he is flawed. That's when he needs me. We have long conversations about this very dichotomy. I've written them down. I'll give them to you—they're around here somewhere."[11]

■   ■   ■

Kirk and Spock were sort of dream images of myself. Two sides of me. I definitely designed it as a love relationship. And I hope that for men . . . who have been afraid of such relationships . . . that they (Spock and Kirk) would encourage them to be able to feel love and affection, true affection . . . love, friendship, and deep respect. That was the relationship I tried to draw. I think I also tried to draw a feeling of belief that very few of us are complete unto ourselves. It's quite a lovely thing, anyplace, where two halves make a whole.[12]

■   ■   ■

Having created Spock and Kirk as two halves of a whole, it is not surprising that the writers and actors involved in portraying them have produced an electrifying relationship that has been the subject of countless essays, books, and

---

[11]These conversations were never found. Even after a thorough search of Gene's private files was conducted, these papers, among others, remain missing to this day.

[12]Gene Roddenberry, in *Star Trek Lives*, by J. Lichtenberg, S. Marshak, and J. Winston, Bantam Books, July 1975, New York, p. 152.

poems, as well as dramatic episodes and films. Leonard Nimoy, the actor who has portrayed Spock for over thirty years (and who at one point became so involved with the psyche of the character that it caused him emotional trauma), describes the relationship as art:

■   ■   ■

I've heard all of these theories about the Spock–Kirk relationship and many, many more. Practically all of them contain a certain validity. . . . As an artist, I try not to anticipate all the various levels of a relationship, because I think if you do, you take the art out of it. . . . I think what it all boils down to is this: here's a man who knows something about me that nobody else knows. Here's a person who understands me in a way that no one else understands me.[13]

Others, who have made a study of the bond between Spock and Kirk, also call it art:

This Spock–Kirk relationship is art. This is the fuel which sustains moral courage, the kind of courage that can drive a mere physical body beyond explainable limits. . . . Each of them triumphs alone. But then from the lonely pinnacles of success, across the deep gorge that separates them, they exchange brief smiles. . . . "Yes, I see you. I know what you've done, and I know what it cost. And I know it was worth it." . . . This is psychological visibility of the rarest and most precious sort. It is the meaning of a friend who is worth the price of one's life.[14]

"What if the problem is an imaginative one?" I ask him.

---

[13]*Ibid.*, pp. 75 and 142.

[14]*Ibid.*, pp. 100 and 101.

"I've always thought Spock lacked a certain quality of imagination."

"He does. He makes up for it somewhat in intuition, though. And if you're going to ask me what the difference is, I don't know. Intuition is, for me, that mysterious process that goes beyond comprehensive, ordered thought—and suddenly you have that shining certainty that it is right, this thing that you have not reasoned out, and you have to . . . to go back and reason it out on a different time scale. I have known things to be certain and have needed to prove to myself that they are certain before I can tell somebody else. It's a flashlight in the dark—that you reveal a thing to yourself and you ask—oh, no, that can't be! But it's there—and you know it. Imagination is something else, something closer to that inspiration we were talking about before—an ability to bring things back from a personal dreamworld and turn them into reality."

"And where is Gene Roddenberry, when Spock and Kirk are both operative?"

"That's when he exists. That's when he really exists—in that state of being I spoke of."

"Do you feel you exist outside that state?"

"Well, other people think so. Sometimes that's enough."

"No, it isn't."

"No—no, you're right, it isn't. What I mean to say is that my life is largely internal. As I suspect yours is. Of course I exist as Gene Roddenberry. That's who I am, here in this world. I do the things I do—and I have a good time doing them. I am a television producer. That demands great attention—application—being present to the daily world and the people in it. I love this world. I love its people. And when I present myself to this world, then that's who I am—outside. Inside, I am a great many things. I'm not just one person. As you are not. But that's what makes us creators. That's what makes us able to meet and to experience so many people as *they* are. And to enter into experiences that we couldn't otherwise have. If we were not multidimensional, we could never be writers. My good friend Arthur C. Clarke has that capacity. Only he keeps it more inside, I think, than I do. I'd like you to meet him. What a conversation the three of us could have. Ray Bradbury, another friend I admire very much, has that capacity. You should meet him too. You'd love him. But most people I know aren't like that. And that's wonderful too. That's just life in all its variety. But—humans have a great need to define themselves. I don't. I don't like to define myself, because as soon as I do, I realize that I have put limitations on how others perceive me."

"You call yourself a humanist. A Jeffersonian. A lot of things. That's definition. That cuts out a lot of other possibilities."

"I don't think I define myself as these things, though. I—I lend myself to them for as long as they work. I'm not one to belong to—to movements and such. I figured out long ago that my wavelength was a very complex wavelength that included things I said and did, and everything about me put out different signals—and that complexity of signals had to emanate from me."

"How do they reach other people? You mean only certain parts will reach other people who can accept them?"

"I will answer that with what you said is a favorite line of yours."

"What?"

" 'I don't know.' " He laughs ruefully, then goes on. "Many people know me as exactly the opposite of how other people know me," he continues. "If you were to talk to my friends and colleagues, you would wonder, why don't they know the Gene Roddenberry I know? With a few friends—a very few—I can be all the people I am, because they recognize me in all these personas. But people generally see me through the more narrow focus of their own experience. The more experience you have of yourself—your selves—the more likely it is that you will reflect that experience and draw others of a similar capacity to you. I mean internal experience, of course. I don't mean traveling and so on, although that could be a catalyst. I know people who travel a great deal and are still very unformed. And I know people who travel very little and are great—brilliant fountains of imagination and ideas."

"Like Isaac Asimov. He's afraid to fly on an airplane and yet takes us on incredible journeys through space."

"Oh, yes. Isaac is one of my good friends. He is one of those brilliant fountains. An incredible man. Do you know him?"

"No. We corresponded a couple of years ago, and in one of his notes to me, he described himself and his books as too cerebral for television. Which is what the network said to you about the first *Star Trek* pilot. I thought it was interesting, especially as we were discussing the similarity between Spock and Daneel."[15]

"You were? How wonderful. Why?"

"Just for fun at the time, although later I wrote a paper about it."

"May I read it?"

"Sure. One of the things I loved in *The Next Generation* is how you incorporated Asimov's term *positronic brain* when describing Data's system."

"Oh, yes. You're one of the few people I know who recognize that. Several years ago, I wrote to Isaac saying,

---

[15]Daneel Olivaw, a robot who first appears in *Caves of Steel*, by Isaac Asimov, part of his Robot trilogy. *Caves of Steel* is published by Ballantine Books, copyright 1953, New York.

'Would you mind if I use the term *positronic brain*?' And he said, 'By all means.'"

"Well, it was very nice to see those two worlds come together. And nice to know that intelligent, creative people of such repute exchange bits of their worlds."

"Most of them that I have met feel that there's no point in saving stuff, because in their lifetime they will do dozens of such things and there's no reason to jealously guard it. I never found Asimov—or Clarke or any of them—answering any note of mine, saying, 'Oh, no—king's x on that—I'm saving it.' Oh, no."

"How much of Isaac Asimov is in *Star Trek*?"

"Quite a fair amount," he says slowly, thinking it over as he speaks. "But I haven't—it is not a copy of any Isaac Asimov work—and it's not a copy of any Isaac Asimov theories, except those that I have adopted with regard to androids. You see, I think quite a useful way to treat androids—or to build androids—is to build them with the three laws of robotics.[16] It presents a sensible thing. There is as much of Isaac Asimov in *Star Trek* as there is of Arthur C. Clarke. And I hope, some of the delightful wit of Ray Bradbury. Any writer that I read and approve, I'm going to borrow from, as I would from any research that I would read and approve."

"Tell me about the creative evolution of *Star Trek*."

"I think I am beginning to know you, and so I think that

---

[16]The Three Laws of Robotics are:

1. A robot may not injure a human being, or, through inaction, allow a human being to come to harm.
2. A robot must obey the orders given it by human beings, except where such orders would conflict with the first Law.
3. A robot must protect its existence, as long as such protection does not conflict with the first or second Law.

Asimov, Isaac, I, *Robot*. Doubleday, New York, 1950.

you aren't asking a historical question—you don't want to know the history of the show."

"No. I know the [general] history of the show, and that information is easily available to anyone else who wants to know about it. I mean how was it impregnated—how was it born?"

"You know, I would just like to say here that I like those images of impregnation and birth. We men often have difficulty applying those terms to ourselves. But we are all male and female inside. Some people recognize that—especially writers, which is why I think my most intimate friends are writers. Others have a terrible time with that notion. That's something I think we should talk about in terms of my philosophy. But to answer your question, and I don't think it is going to be an adequate answer: as those things happen, it sprung forth with rather full strength."

"Like Minerva, from the head of Jupiter."

"Oh, yes, quite like that. As a matter of fact, in addition to writing a script, I wrote a whole treatment of how *Star Trek* should work. I wrote what I saw in my place of—of contemplation. I guess it's that thing I said before: they were there. Perhaps I am an adoptive parent, to continue the analogy."

"Who are the original parents?"

"I don't know. That very loose definition of—of inspiration, I guess. I don't say that *Star Trek* was created in an instant. No—it evolved. And a good many people contributed to its evolution. But the overall idea came rather—well, it just came! You know, over the years, I've used several tricks, and it may mean that at different times, you need different tricks to keep your mind working. One of my favorites is to concentrate on something about our world that annoys me—so that I get sufficiently moved, so that I want to write about how, in the *Star Trek* world, it's done differently. Those things usually have to deal with the things we talked about today—relationships and technology, and openness and so on. I don't start writing immediately. I talk to friends; I try to put my mind to where theirs is. I try to find out what went wrong for them, or what may have gone very, very right. Having done that, I pursue that line, until I start thinking consecutively, in a pattern, until I seem to be connected with that mind. Not in a fancy way, but . . . just in a useful way." He stops and searches my face for a few seconds. In a few days, I will know why. "Anyway," he continues, "for instance, I know Spock so well that I have actually turned out pages of dialogue with me and Spock, and I say, 'Why do you think this way?' And he answers. With Spock, it comes very close to telepathy. But that is because I am Spock. I have some very good Spock/Roddenberry writing that I've never published, and don't think I ever shall. It gave away a lot about us and our relationship." He stops again, cocks his head to one side, and smiles ruefully. "On the other hand, that's what we're doing, isn't it? I'd like you to read my Spock papers. And I promised I'd find them for you."

■　■　■

I never knew how his mind worked. What he said when he said it made absolute sense, and he evidently had the ability to think large in no time. He was kind of— Spocky.

—*Robert H. Justman*

■　■　■

He reminds me of some melodramatic portraits of Jupiter I have seen sometimes, sitting so still. I imagine him to be in the act of creation—in the process of generation. Physically large, mentally vast, and cosmically quiet, he has a paradoxical presence: imperious and self-effacing, as though he were winking in and out of existence, in and out of time. In reality, he is declining, and his stillness may simply be vacant rest. And yet, he is an enormously busy man, with many claims on his time—even at this stage of his life, in which he is clearly not well. When I ask him later what his schedule is for the next day, he says, "Oh," in a surprised voice. "I want to serve you." He remarks that he thinks we will spend many months together, in companionable silence, in vigorous conversation, on the set, in the house. Unstructured time, dream time, he says.

■　　■　　■

We have only a few weeks left.

■　　■　　■

"I learned something from a person long ago," he continues. "When you've got free time, imagine emergencies that you will someday have to deal with. When you're taking a long flight, imagine this going wrong, or that going wrong."

I start laughing. He looks startled.

"I have enough trouble just being comfortable on an airplane, without imagining disasters," I tell him.

"But what would you do? What would be your first move?" he replies in genuine consternation, and adds as an afterthought, "And it's a delightful game."

"Well . . ." I am still laughing. "I don't know about delightful. Useful, maybe."

"Oh—useful, yes. Very useful. It's delightful too. It's nothing more than a game that you play with yourself."

"But you're not afraid of airplanes."

"No."

"Well, I am."

"Well," he says convincingly, "you wouldn't be, after you'd played that game."

But he has survived the reality of that game. Having been

on a plane which crashed in the Syrian desert in 1947, he may have been saved from reality by imagination.

■   ■   ■

It is a bright morning. We have been sitting by the pool, talking for two hours. He has been telling me stories of his childhood. We were both precocious and voracious readers as children, with heads full of heroes. I ask him who his are.

"Well, I have always said Captain Horatio Hornblower was a great hero of mine—and in some ways, he still is. Yes, he is, and Sherlock Holmes—but I have found in so many, many people evidence of heroism, the ability to perform heroic acts, that I think I have people I admire, rather than heroes. Of course I retain those early heroes, Hornblower and—and, well, I was going to say Lincoln, President Lincoln, but if you're talking about my *real personal heroes*, I am surprised to find myself saying that they are all fictional characters."

"How interesting. So are mine. Why is that, do you think?"

"Well, probably because we are idealists, you and I. No one can ever really live up to the heroic ideal, can they? And so— they have to be fictional."

"Oh, maybe. I was thinking more that when you read a book, you know a fictional character—you're inside his head—you know the way he thinks and feels. So you can be more certain that he is a hero inside before you take him as a personal ideal. Whereas with living people, that isn't possible, at least not usually. There are a few exceptions."

"Yes, I think that's true for me too. Who are your exceptions?" he asks curiously.

"My dad. A couple of other people whom I've been fortunate enough to know well enough to understand an inner heroism. But the others are all fictional. One is a combination of both."

"How fascinating," he says. "A combination of both. Who?"

I look at him in exasperation.

"Oh," he says with a swift descent into shyness. "Thank you."

■　　■　　■

"Do you know," he says later on that afternoon, as if it were unthinkably wondrous that people should want to meet him, "I've been fortunate to have been able to meet most of my exceptions—the people who are real-life heroes to me: Arthur C. Clarke and Asimov and the fellows at NASA and, oh, so many others—people who may not be as well known to you, but I have to say that in this respect, my dreams have come true. I think our heroes help define us, help us choose the attributes we wish to have—the qualities that may very well be within us—*are* within us, or we wouldn't pick those particular people for heroes." He glances at a small *Enterprise* on his desk. "But *Star Trek* is what best defines me—*if* you see it for what it is."

"You are your own hero?"

"Yes, in a curious way. Because I create—or rather develop—the characters with qualities I may lack or lack strength in, and they become my heroes. Yes, in the sense that I am *Star Trek*, I am my own hero."

"You keep saying that. Is that really what you mean? I mean, *Star Trek* is also the studio, the actors, directors, the scriptwriters—it's a TV show."

"I see you're playing devil's advocate. I think you know exactly what I mean."

"You are *Star Trek*. And the TV show is a manifestation of *Star Trek*. A manifestation, in fact, of you?"

"Yes."

"Well, that's defining yourself, isn't it? The kind of thing you say you never do."

He smiles. "I'm hungry. Let's go get something to eat." We

90

make our way through the house, slowly. Just before we reach the front door, he stops and looks down into my eyes.

"I really am *Star Trek,*" he says quietly.

■   ■   ■

This self-identification with the entity he had created permeated our conversations. Whatever we said, wherever we went, whatever we did together and apart, it was an Angelus, ringing out regularly and with ponderous acclaim, acclaim, acclaim—and claiming all who would know him to seek him through this one phrase. "I am *Star Trek*"—a *crie de coeur* of surprising intensity—"I am *Star Trek*"—a generic, primordial, insistent refrain.

To hear it was to hear Cathy screaming into the moor wind, "I am Heathcliffe"—to peer into the burning bush and listen through the ears of Moses, "I am Yahweh." I had watched the shows again and again, looking into a television world pierced with advertisements but touched with the secret that despite its flaws has kept millions glued to their sets for (then) twenty-five years. I didn't find him; or rather, what I found seemed to stop short of the rumpled, vigorous man whom so many called "visionary." At times, his obsession was frightening—a fanatical light would enter his eyes, then fade, as quickly as it came. I had been to conventions like a visitor at a zoo, watching, at times, a sad parade of people munch through their sustenance of T-shirts, phasers, memorabilia, comic books, and thought, *Get a life,* as William Shatner unkindly and truthfully said on *Saturday Night Live.* Or was this a life—or Life—a media salvation for the internally inept? A prepackaged fifty-minute philosophy, beginning with "love thy neighbor" and ending with not a whimper but the big bang? It disturbed me, this insistence on definition— which he claimed he eschewed—this convenient explana- tion for being. Something didn't fit.

91

I had posed a question a few days before, about which he said he was still thinking. The question was this: "The words *organized religion* seem to bring a little fire into your reflective, calm response to life. Why are you so against it? Isn't it the same as organized *Star Trek*? There are sheep in every facet of life." He said he would think about it, and now considers the question seriously on our way to lunch.

"I think you have a point," he says unwillingly. "It makes me sad to see anyone latch onto anything—for the wrong reasons. But you know, you have to look further than that. Some of these wonderful people who wear uniforms and Spock ears and so on, well—humans like symbols, mementos of what they love, and while you or I may choose different symbols, or none at all, what we share with these fans is a deep conviction of the value of the principles these symbols represent. They are often the ones who know what *Star Trek* really is. And some of these folks are just there to have a good time. They dress up because they like to have fun with these things, to feel like they are a part of a world that accepts them. They're not misfits, as the media often makes out; they're people whose environment perhaps does not allow for some of the things we most treasure in *Star Trek*— individuality, difference, diversity. They may be at a stage in their life that it makes them feel good to go to a convention. It's not a place of thou-shalt-nots. The only thou-shalt-not in *Star Trek* is interfering with anyone's right to be who they are. I don't say that there aren't some very sad and lonely people who go to conventions; some people may use it as an escape. But the great majority of fans go because it's fun. They meet other people who appreciate the *Star Trek* future. And they find a little encouragement to go off and explore something inside them, some dream they may not have a chance to discover any other way. And of course most of the people who watch *Star Trek* and appreciate it for what it is don't go to conventions—astronauts, professors, heads of government, scientists—thinkers—people like you who both think and dream. The difference between that and a religion is that in religion, the dream is already created for them."

I open my mouth to argue, but he anticipates it. "We're all in different stages of realization," he says. "Besides, here we are."

.   ■   .

The Hotel Bel Air always reminds me of a cathedral, in its hushed reverence for its own gods. Corridors and arches, sanctuaries and silence, protect its patrons from the mundane. It is beautiful: its outdoor patio is canopied this July day with purple flowers that drift noiselessly onto the table. A solitary blossom comes to rest on Gene's head. This time, he lets me order—and as we wait for what is certain to be a perfect and picturesque lunch, I look around. Everyone crackles with awareness, eyes darting from table to table to see who is with whom and to speculate why. Gene looks only at the table and me, years of celebrity status having taught him that catching someone's eye is inadvisable if one wishes to remain uninterrupted.

"So—you are *Star Trek*," I say, admiring the flower perched on the rough silver thatch of his hair, like an unexpected Easter egg in a winter nest.

"Yes. And I can see that that statement annoys you, and I want to know why."

"Because it isn't enough. It's like holding out your arm or leg, pointing to it, and saying, 'This is me—this defines who I am.'"

He smiles his charming smile. "Well, it isn't an arm or leg—it's my heart."

"That's the kind of statement that can be quoted forever and thrill thousands, and believe me, I know it's true, but there's something missing—a greater truth, perhaps. You can't sum yourself up in so small a package."

"*Small?*" he says, outraged for an instant. Heads turn. He lowers his voice. "*Star Trek* isn't small. It's a whole universe of possibility. It's . . . it's the greatest panorama of possibility we have on television today."

"On television, yes. But what happens to you when the studio doors close, when the TV gets turned off? Who are you then—a blank screen?"

He looks at me keenly and starts to brush back his hair.

"Don't do that," I say quickly. He gives me a puzzled glance. "There's a flower on your head."

"Oh." He smiles sweetly, with the air of having been given a gift. "How lovely."

Lunch is served, predictably pretty, a seductive, artful blend of color, form, and illusion. The waiter glances briefly at Gene's head, then at me, in a slightly accusing manner. Gene intercepts the look, seemingly without raising his eyes from the plate. "She likes it there," he says, with the same sweet smile. *If this were a movie,* I think, *that would be the cue for the waiter to raise his eyebrows and exit with a slight air of disapproval.* He does so.

"I thought you loved *Star Trek*," Gene remarks in no particular tone, picking up his fork.

"I do."

"Then . . ."

"But I don't define who I am by the fact that I love it. And I can't accept that you do. Instinctively, you don't refer to yourself as the creator of *Star Trek*. Other people do. But you always refer to yourself as a writer. What I'm trying to get to is who you are, beyond what you do. Otherwise, what I hear is that cinema character of Woody Allen's in *The Purple Rose of Cairo* who, when he jumps off the screen into real life, thinks a kiss is followed by a fade-out."

He leans back and starts to laugh. He laughs so heartily that slight frowns appear on the careful faces of those at nearby tables. *It must be some kind of sacrilege,* I think—*a man with a flower on his head, laughing in what amounts to church.* The flower falls off.

"A kiss, followed by a fade-out," he repeats. "Well, I certainly have never thought that!"

"You know what I mean."

"Followed by fade-out," he says again, still chuckling. "That's good." He begins to eat happily. "All right. Would it be better if I said 'Star Trek is me'?"

"It might be nearer the truth. Look, I told you when we started out that this book is not essentially about *Star Trek.* It's about you. You said you were happy about that. And all I hear you say is—"

"I think I said I was elated. Not happy. Elated."

"Whatever. So, can we stop talking about *Star Trek,* just for a little while, and start talking about you?"

"Oh—I would love to. But you know, I am a private man, and I am so used to giving public answers that I suppose I keep forgetting that it really is me you're interested in. Most people are interested in me only because of *Star Trek.* And I'm happy that they are. I think I'm trying to be self-revealing—and I don't know how much or how little to say about myself. I think I must be more courageous, and perhaps it is time—of course it is time—to say some things about myself that it may not have been right to say before. I'm sorry. What should I say? Help me."

"Why don't you tell me what it is, when you're not working on, thinking about, representing, in any way, *Star Trek,* that you do think about."

He stops eating and looks away from me—out into the distance for so long that the lettuce starts to curl. When he finally turns back to me, his face is noticeably different.

"Majel," he says.

■   ■   ■

"I think about her all the time now." He goes on, slowly, haltingly, listening carefully to his own words. "I daydream about her." He stops. "Nobody knows this." He picks up his fork, puts it down, lets his hands fall helplessly into his lap. "Are you going to . . . ? No—that's a stupid question. I'm sorry. Of course you are."

"Not if you don't want me to."

He sighs. "Yes. Put it in. She deserves it," he adds, disconsolately. "And in any case, it's true."

"Why does it make you react so somberly to say such a lovely thing?"

"I don't know. Maybe because it is so private. Maybe because I've spent so much time convincing myself—and others—otherwise."

"I don't understand."

"Majel is . . ." A thousand expressions cross his face. He begins again. "Majel is . . . do you know why I asked you to come and stay with us at the house?"

"Because we couldn't get any work done at the studio. Because you said if I was to paint a portrait of you in words, then I would need to live with you and your family, do the things you did, be with you in your private life."

"Yes. All those things—and something else."

"You said, 'I want you to meet my wife. She'll love you.' "

"Yes—and she does. She doesn't know it yet, but she does. But it wasn't just a conventional invitation. I also hoped you'd love her. Not just for her sake. I also have a selfish reason."

"Oh?"

"Yes, well—now can you see what I mean?"

"No."

"All right. Finish my sentence: 'Majel is . . .' "

I open my mouth. A hundred words come to mind— perhaps a thousand. Instantly arising, instantly discarded. Nothing comes out.

"You see?" he says.

"But, Gene—you've been married to her for over twenty years. I've known her only a few weeks."

"Doesn't matter. I couldn't describe her twenty years ago, and I can't now. I was hoping you might."

"Why?"

"Because you . . . see things."

"What does this have to do with the way you think? Who you are?"

"It has everything to do with it. Everything. Oh, this is a very difficult thing."

I feel I am treading on private territory. I'm not here to write a tell-all book. I begin to retreat.

"Perhaps we can come back to this subject later," I begin.

"No," he says firmly. It sounds like an order. "No. This is something I have to say."

His left thumb begins to move rapidly across his index finger in a series of never-ending cycles. It is a gesture I have come to recognize as signaling deep, unexpressed emotion. I had told him once that it was his "magic lantern" gesture—except that the genie always wants to get into the lamp rather than out of it.

"She was my best friend," he goes on. I notice the word *was* but do not say anything. "We were great friends, you know—long before we were lovers." I nod, not wanting to voice any question, to engender any thought he prefers not to express. "We talked about everything. Including *Star Trek*. Especially *Star Trek*. She would sit with me for hours, discussing this character or that—and props and so on. It was my world, not hers, and yet she shared it so intimately." He looks at me for a moment and sees in my face what I am thinking, answers it accurately. "Oh, but it was harder for her. As it would be for anyone. It was something I had thought up; it was a dream I had. This was not something she would naturally gravitate to, this crazy notion, this oddball guy. She made a terrible leap of faith in me—I mean terrible in the archaic sense—wonderful, frightening. Into that cosmic Oz, as you like to call it. In a sense, she helped form it—not create it—I did that—but shape it. And once she made that leap, she never looked back. She stood for whatever I stood for. I guess she became part of my dreamworld, which is why I said I daydream about her. Well, we all have our own private dreamworlds, don't we?"

"And?"

He looks at me levelly. "Sometimes," he says slowly, "sometimes . . . I feel . . . I can't get into hers."

▪   ▪   ▪

Later, much later, I will ask him, "Who besides you has done the most to develop the *Star Trek* world?"

He will answer, "Majel."

▪   ▪   ▪

Who besides Gene has done the most to develop the *Star Trek* world? Oh, Majel, of course; she was there from the beginning—she's still there. She's half the reason there *is* a fandom out there—and Gene's the other half.

—William Ware Theiss

Majel.

—Christopher Knopf

Majel.

—E. Jack Neuman

Well, Majel, of course.

—Robert H. Justman

Majel. And she's never given enough credit.

—an anonymous friend

Majel, obviously. She was a major contributor to keeping *Star Trek* alive.

—Sam Rolfe

■　　■　　■

I already know this, of course. Before deciding to do a book on Gene Roddenberry, I attended several conventions, watched many of the actors on stage, took notes from a distance while those who gave autographs gave them. At each of these conventions, I asked fans who their favorite character was. The answers varied widely. When asked who their favorite actor/actress was, the universal favorite was Majel, and the most common reason given was "She *cares.*"

■　　■　　■

The waiter comes to ask if we need anything. Gene seems to wake up. He remembers his food and starts to eat. I feel a curious energy emanating from him—a surreality of hope and longing. It feels like a plea. It suddenly seems very important not to say anything. When, still in silence, we finish lunch, he shifts in his chair. "I'm very tired," he says. "Let's go home."

■　　■　　■

He takes a nap. Whenever I return from a visit to the Roddenberrys, I sleep off and on for about twenty-four hours. But while there, a kind of writer's energy replaces sleep. I go into the TV room to find Majel. "Oh, there you are," she says as though I were late for an appointment. "Come here. I'm going to show you how to make hats. You're finished with

Gene, aren't you?" I think how impossible it is to ever be finished with Gene, and I sit down obediently amidst a cacophony of beads, pins, glitter, glue. There are straw hats everywhere—plain, half finished, complete. She sells them at conventions and *Star Trek* cruises, I later find out, and am astonished. Why would a millionaire's wife spend hours making hats to sell at a price far below any hope of breaking even? I give a mental shrug and just assume that she does it because she wants to. There doesn't seem to be any other reason. But there is. The fans like them. She holds up a completed hat. "See? This is what we're going to do. What do you think?"

"Tacky," I say, not thinking, and am instantly regretful.

Majel lets out a peal of laughter. "You're such a character," she exclaims delightedly. "Now look. First you cut a length of ribbon . . ."

I'm *a character,* I think to myself, watching her immediate, intense absorption in the task of explaining. Her movements are Data-like, syncopated, accurate, simulated, as though she were wearing someone else's body and is not quite used to it. Her blouse is matted with cat hair, her legs mapped with scratches from the rose garden. There are two pairs of glasses on her wild head. She holds up a length of ribbon. "Isn't this pretty?" She looks up at me. There is glue on her face. *It's the eyes,* I think. Enormous, wild, luminous, clear, they *seem* to promise an entrance into that dreamworld he says he can't find.

"What do you think about?" I ask her.

"Whatever I'm doing," she replies without hesitation. But I can see that she is canny, aware.

"What if you're not doing anything?"

"Oh, I'm always doing something," she says. "Now pay attention."

We work for a while. I am hopeless at the task. She speaks

to me kindly and slowly as if to a retarded child. "Now, bend this wire. . . . Now, count these loops. . . ." All the time, her antennae are up, searching for a hidden motive in my question. She says nothing about it, but I know, somehow, that she will return to the question. She does.

"I *don't* think," she says. "I really don't. I'm not an intelligent person. I'm very shallow. I like being shallow. I like fun and laughter. I'm not serious like you . . . and Gene," she adds after a pause. On her face is a curious mixture of expressions. For some inexplicable reason, I remember a look on Spock's face, in "Amok Time," an unlikely combination of defiance, defense, dignity, fear. She pretends not to wait for my comment, rubs a nasty scratch on her leg.

■　■　■

We have known each other for a month.

■　■　■

"Oh, I think that kind of camouflage is the creation of a very intelligent person," I say. "But nice try."

She flicks the television on and snatches the hat away. "Oh, dear—it's all wrinkled. You have to cut the ribbon so it *fits.*"

■　■　■

Later that evening, after dinner, when the three of us are sitting in the TV room, she jumps up in the middle of a sentence long forgotten now. "You haven't seen my office, have you?"

"No."

"I want you to see it. Come with me."

She continues as we make our way to the basement. "I don't let many people come down here, but I want you to see it." She flips on a light. We are in a jungle. Or a dream. The walls, the ceiling, the window shades, are painted in an astonishing mural of flora and fauna—intense color, form, and primeval energy. There is more clear space on the Sistine Chapel ceiling than in this profusion of paint. The eyes of animals wink at us from behind their mythical leaves. There is life everywhere. Her eyes turn green. They follow mine to the leopard-skin carpet.

"Fake," she says righteously. "I'm an animal activist."

(A year later, her mother tries to give me a fur coat. "Majel won't let me wear it; it's just hanging in the closet. Would you like it?" I thank her, decline, and tell Majel later: "Give her a break—she's eighty-two. Those animals were probably killed before you were born."

"Well, they shouldn't have been," she retorts. "Go away. You're bothering me."

"But it's her, not you. And it's her coat."

"She can wear it. I just won't go anywhere with her when she does."

"Majel . . ."

"Look, if you *stand* for something, *you stand for it.*"

At this moment, we have not yet been through that year—that year of grief and mourning, private tears and public appearances, conversations and revelations—the year following Gene's death, the year that makes this sisterly exchange possible.)

We sit down. I look uneasily over my shoulder. She laughs. "They don't bite. Gorgeous, isn't it?"

"Wild."

"That's the point."

I wonder what the point of this tête-à-tête will be. It is not long in coming. She begins to talk about Gene. What she says mirrors my earlier conversation with him. I feel that I have stepped from Oz into the *Jungle Book,* ending up in *Alice Through the Looking Glass.* I feel certain that *Romeo and Juliet* is next. Suddenly, her Data-like movements fall into grace:

she inhabits herself for a few moments. Her hands move from gesticulation to repose. She puts them on her lap and then, in a series of never-ending circles, her thumb begins to move rapidly across her index finger. I look closely. Her right thumb. Mirror image.

She wants to make sure I know who he is, from her point of view—not to make a mistake and think that there is anything about him that is not justifiable. That whatever he says, he has a right to say. That if there is any criticism of her, he is right, if not in fact, then in the stating of it. She lowers her head, as if for the guillotine, and begins to tell me why. I listen. There is innocence in her neck. What she says, I don't remember now. If I did, I would not record it. This is Gene's book. All I remember is that I have never witnessed such a curious lack of ego—and such self-abnegation—in all my life. "If Gene is *Star Trek*, then Majel is Gene," I will write in my notebook later that night and not know why. In the middle of her uncomfortable litany, I stop her. "Majel, I don't know you well enough to be hearing this. I don't have the right."

I know this is a false statement before I have finished saying it.

"Yes, you do," she says, echoing Gene's own words. "Chemistry gives you the right."

I do not tell her of our lunchtime conversation.

She never asks me.

■   ■   ■

In the years following these conversations, I have heard many pontificate on the marriage of Majel and Gene, each certain that she (for in each case, it was a she) knew the inner workings of Gene's heart, but none of whom knew—or had the slightest possibility of knowing—Majel's. They seem curiously arrogant, possessive, jealous, insecure—and firmly attest that the marriage was a failure. I find out, in these two years, from his male friends, that this attitude typifies the women whom Gene drew to himself for his own, odd reasons—women who claim him as a badge of identification, as if he were a dog tag. It is for that reason that I first discarded their testimony, the second reason being what Gene said in the pages that follow. The substantive reason, of course, is that in the months that I stayed with Majel and Gene, I saw an obsessive, passionate bond that was beyond understanding—a raw, painful bridge between them that seemed to have been built by strips of their own skin. The efforts I saw between them to hold it together were almost too painful to watch. I did not understand that relationship then, nor do I now. They seemed to oppose each other because they existed to each other. Had they been indifferent, I suppose they would have lived in peace.

■　　■　　■

One day, Gene talks about Majel for nearly two hours. I think and think for months afterward about all that he has said. What I end up with is this: Like many writers, he carries a population around inside him—ideas, fancies, notions, characters, theories, possibilities, dreams. They buzz constantly with opposing suggestions, contradictory philosophies, conflicting needs. They make claims upon him, demand of him that they be given life. They ask him questions he cannot answer, force him to confront his own limitations. He feels obligated to acknowledge their validity, to give time and attention to their incessant needs, and—what is worse, far worse for him—to make choices. In every choice he makes, about which character will live and which will be forever confined to the purgatory of partial existence, he hears a scream from those who cannot be brought to life. Every decision in favor of one is denial to another. Choice is his nemesis, in life as well as art. It is the hardest thing he has to do, he tells me. There is one word in his vocabulary which he hates above all others. That word is *no*.

■　　■　　■

Life, like writing, is making choices. You can never know what might have been. It is a drama—you're in conflict with your environment, and your environment consists of other people and their needs. You consist of your needs.

—*Robert H. Justman*

■　　■　　■

I hear many stories from those who worked closely with him. He has no trouble saying no to anything that will not be of benefit to *Star Trek*. But he finds it almost impossible to say no to people in a personal capacity. In fact, I am told often, that task is one of the few he delegates. Several people recount a particularly revealing anecdote about someone who worked in a very minor capacity on *Star Trek: The Next Generation*, "helping with research." When she asked Gene for an opportunity to do more on the show, Gene sent her to see Bob Justman.

While she was en route, Gene picked up the phone and called Bob on the set. "Say no," Gene instructed him. Justman recalls that "Gene had no intention of actually hiring this woman but, characteristically, was unable to say no."

In anything that does not touch *Star Trek*, *no* is a word that connects him to fear. He is afraid to say it. What might have been beckons him. In this, he is connected to Majel so deeply that in this two-hour monologue he calls her a saving grace, a metaphor that is not lost on me and that he hastily tries to change to another phrase. But he can find none. That is what she is. Brave in the face of *no*, philosophical about what might have been, "she lives entirely in the present," he says.

"My body could have married anyone," he remarks, "but *I* had to marry Majel." I am again reminded of Woody Allen, who once said that his body was just something he used to carry his brain around in. When Gene says *I*, he disembodies whatever constitutes that which he is from that which he appears to be. Clearly, his detachment from himself is profound. He is the sort of person who, if injured, will say, "My leg is bleeding" rather than "I am bleeding." He attaches almost no importance to his body, except as an instrument of pleasure. It has no intrinsic value. When I ask him what it is about Majel that saves him, he begins a discourse on infinite diversity. I do not know yet what he means. In the months that follow, I will find out. But that will be in the future. Right now, he says, his own complexity tires him. Majel doesn't. She is free of that whimpering population inside, and because of that, he finds freedom in her.

What he draws from her is nothing he recognizes—it is the very lack of internal divisiveness in which he rests. He needs her, he tells me. He needs her to be who she is, and the one thing that he can count on is that she will always be it. She is real, he adds proudly, as if it were a virtue not to be imaginary—and looks puzzled that he said it. Of what that reality consists, he cannot define. He knows only that it somehow absorbs the infinite diversity boiling inside him. Others understand parts of him profoundly, satisfy one or several of the people he is inside. But only Majel makes that "terrible leap of faith" and stands for whatever he stands for, whether she understands it or not. Once, in this conversation, he mentions *Star Trek* fans. Only Majel really cares in the same way he cares about fandom, he says.

■　　■　　■

How deeply she cares is evident to me a few months after Gene's death. We are sitting in Gene's study, reading thousands of condolence letters, which pour in daily. Among them is a letter requesting something with Gene Roddenberry's signature on it, to be given away as a memento to someone at a memorial gathering of fans. In the corner are boxes of Starfleet certificates on which Gene's original signature has been reproduced. When it is suggested that one of these be sent, Majel refuses. "Those are *copies* of his signature, not his real signature," she says. Her personal assistant points out that fans are sensible people who realize that a man in Gene Roddenberry's position cannot spend hundreds of hours a week signing certificates—and that a reproduced autograph is acceptable. Majel is adamant. "Somewhere out there," she says, looking across Gene's desk, out the window, and into a world that only she sees, "is a person, a human being who will treasure this thing he or she has been given, believing it to be Gene's own writing. Someone who treasures *Gene*. And they are going to *get* Gene." She spends a good part of the afternoon hunting for an appropriate item. When, several hours later, she emerges with a scrap of paper on which for some reason Gene had written his name, she is quietly triumphant. "There!" she says. "This is *real*."

■　■　■

"We still haven't talked about fear," I say to Gene when I join him in the garden the next day.

"What do you think about sex?" he asks.

"Is this another Gene Roddenberry diversionary tactic?"

"No. No. I would like to know. Because I have a statement to make about that, and I'd like to hear what you think."

"I think it is not an intimate act. It can be made intimate— by engaging in it with someone with whom you are already intimate, or becoming so. But in and of itself, it's a human function, like all other human functions—resembling hunger, I suppose, the most. I certainly don't think it is a way to achieve intimacy. I mean, eating can be an intimate act, if it is with the right person. Or it can just be a way of filling a need to survive. Robert Heinlein created a culture in which eating was the most intimate act, and these little creatures go into cubicles or recesses in the walls and turn their backs on everyone else when they eat. That was in *Space Cadet,* one of my favorite science-fiction books."

"Do you know that that is one of the most significant books in my life!" he exclaims. "Let's talk about that next. But—what *do* you think intimacy is?"

"I think talking with someone, really communicating deeply—getting inside that other person—is an intimate act. . . ."

"Well, getting inside someone is also sex."

"From a male point of view, yes. Intimacy is also letting someone enter you, not just at a level of warmth and goodwill and friendship, not even of love, but at the core—the place one survives from. Sex is a *metaphor* of that kind of intimacy; it is not the intimacy itself. It's a—a physical manifestation, at best, of what you say *Star Trek* is all about: contact."

"Sex is a metaphor of intimacy—not the other way around?" He seems to want to be very sure of my meaning.

"As I see it, yes."

"I think that qualifies as a lovely statement. And I thought you might say something like that. It's something I've always believed. The separation of sex and intimacy between men and women is something I try to portray in *Star Trek.*"

"Where? When? I haven't seen much evidence of it."

"Of course you have. It's there."

"If you mean Captain Kirk . . ."

"Oh, forget Kirk. I'm talking about *The Next Generation*. We have a very lovely possibility there between Riker and Deanna Troi. They are friends, first and foremost, and then they have this sexual component. And they can choose to utilize that component—act on it—or not. But it's not a romance. You must have noticed that. I hope it comes through."

"I think it does sometimes. But I thought I might be seeing something that wasn't there, again."

"Oh, no—you're seeing what's there."

"But other times, it seems like a traditional romance."

"Well, it's not supposed to be. I wrote it as a sort of prototype relationship, a friendship between the opposite sexes carried to its fullest capacity."

"How does that differ from romance?"

"I think you've answered that question in what you said about sex, but you're probably not relating it to my statement. Romance is a product of not knowing each other. Friendship develops when you know each other. And then, if it's possible—and sadly, it usually isn't—you can have intimacy. Sexual or not. It doesn't matter. Sex is not germane to intimacy, as you said. Two men can be more intimate than a man and his wife. Or two women. Or a man and a woman who understand one another, perhaps share one another's dreams, but have no wish to live together or share their bodies with one another."

"Well," I say, "I don't think it's all that clear in the Riker–Troi case. It often looks awfully like plain old American romance to me. I think you did better with Kirk and Spock."[17]

"Well, that may be because it is easier for me. I myself am

---

[17]Since this conversation, there have been several episodes that outline the Riker–Troi relationship more clearly.

so intimate with them. And then, it's hard to portray non-physical intimacy between members of the opposite sex—especially between such attractive people. It can so easily look like what it isn't."

"So when do two people marry?"

"I think they don't, in a perfect world. I don't think there's that kind of mutual possession. Marriage in the form that it is now cannot possibly continue into the future. That's why we have so little of it in *Star Trek*."

"There is no marrying or giving in marriage in *Star Trek*, as in heaven, as your favorite book says?"

"Yes. I think if we all lived in my *Star Trek* world, it would be pretty close to heaven. You see, the studio executives and so on think that our people are single, so that there are romantic possibilities for them. So the audience can identify with the current love interest, as they call it, each week. But that was not my intention. My idea was to portray a world in which people are developed enough as humans to be sufficient unto themselves and in which they had a wonderful world of human and alien contact to explore. They don't remain single, from my point of view, in order to satisfy some romantic need on the part of the audience. And I hope that the people who watch *Star Trek* may see something in this. We also have many families on board—traditional families and some nontraditional families, which we haven't had an opportunity to bring out yet. But those are just choices—made out of many possibilities. That's something I would really like to get into more on our show." He adds thoughtfully, "Of course, heroes on television—and in the movies—were traditionally never married—or even 'taken,' engaged and so on. That's an old maxim. Oh, they always got the girl, but . . ."

"When they do, the movie ends. Technicolor kiss."

"And fade-out." He laughs heartily. "Yes, the movie always used to end just when it was getting interesting, from that point of view. Things are somewhat different now, thank God."

"How does this relate to your own life?"

"Oh, it does. I believe it. And within the bounds of what it takes to maintain a happy marriage, it's what I do. I practice what I preach. There may be times when I feel like 'dipping my wick,' and I do so. When it's right. When it feels good. People may say, 'Oh, that Gene Roddenberry—he's no good; he's an unfaithful husband.' I say, unfaithful to what?"

"Majel, surely."

"No. Not at all. People aren't concerned in their deepest selves about Majel. They're concerned about themselves, their rules and so on. They mean I am unfaithful to the ideal—*their ideal* of marriage. They don't want to consider another ideal. They may be afraid. They may condemn me for breaking a vow they think I made. Whereas in fact, I didn't make it. I could never adhere to an agreement that deprived me of myself. Majel and I have our own agreement. I would be false—a false person—if I did make any other kind of agreement. And I would be a false person if my wife didn't know who I am, what I do."

"And is this 'wick dipping' ever an intimate act?"

"You mean, outside my marriage? No. I have varying degrees of friendship with people—I am involved in more kinds of love than I could possibly relate—but no, I can't say that I feel intimate—in the manner we are speaking of—with anyone with whom I enjoy that particular pleasure."

"What do you suppose they feel?"

"Oh, I suppose some of them feel they have been intimate with me. Perhaps their capacity is filled. Some of them may just like to feel that they've fucked Gene Roddenberry. And that's okay too. But I've never given the impression that a roll in the sack is the key to Gene Roddenberry's soul. At least I hope I haven't. And then, sometimes, you know, it's just a human thing you do. Someone feels lonely, or they need a bit of loving—or they just need some confirmation that they can be someone who is attractive to someone else."

"So at those times, it's a kindness—a service to the neglected, the lonely?" I am having a hard time keeping my face serious.

"Yes, yes, I think it is," Gene says, then adds, "Sometimes it is. Other times, it's simply a way to love life—to love the life in myself—and the life, the humanity in someone else. Some people may think that's just my way of justifying—"

"Is it?"

"No. I don't need to justify my actions in that regard."

"With whom are you most intimate?"

"Spock."

"Besides Spock. A real person."

"Spock is a real person to me. He doesn't always live in the world you and I inhabit, but he's a real person."

"Sorry. I'll rephrase the question. Besides Spock, with whom are you or have you been most intimate?"

"I don't think I can give one answer to that. There are several. Majel, certainly." He names a few others—all men. I begin to see that by intimacy, he means an ability to reach him, while he is reaching for something else. Or to reach into that something else with him.

"No women?" I ask.

"Oh, I love women. I am a fan of women. I have many wonderful female friends. But as far as intimacy goes, they never seem to remain sufficiently detached."

"Your definition of intimacy includes detachment?"

"You sound surprised. Doesn't yours? I would have thought, from our discussion at breakfast this morning, that it would."

"Yes, it does, but so few people understand that a relationship between oneself and another is subordinate to the relationship between one and oneself."

"Well, I'm not so few people, I'm so many people!" He laughs. "No—that merging is a wonderful thing. I seek it. But it is not something through which you live your life. Actually, a lot of people espouse these views. But they just can't do it. I don't know why, but they just can't. Perhaps most people need something that you and I find in ourselves. One of humanity's great failings, intimacy. And a hard question to answer with regard to myself."

"Would it help to ask who knows most about you—well, not you, your inner self?"

"Well, at the moment, I'd have to say you do."

"And when the moment has passed?"

"I didn't say, 'for the moment.' I said, 'at the moment.' It's all these questions you ask—these glorious, difficult, goddamn questions. And the answers I have to come up with—have to somehow find. And that is true of the answers we decide to publish—and the ones we don't." He smiles. "Of course it's more complex than that. As I said, we may be of the same species. And don't ask me what species, because I don't know. But we may help each other find out. Oh, yes—I think we will always remain wonderful, intimate friends. I'm counting on it."

"You realize," I say, "that when this is published, then whoever reads it will be, in effect, an intimate."

"How wonderful. What a thought. I will be an intimate of humanity. What a lovely—what a magnificent—thing to contemplate. Thank you. I think I'll go and have a rest; I'd like to be by myself for a while and think about that. Thank you."

■   ■   ■

"I've thought about that last idea we had, and I'm a little blue," he says later that day.

"Why?"

"Well, it's the whole idea of contact again. People are intimates because they reveal themselves to each other, or because they are capable of revealing themselves to each other, even if they don't choose to at first. That lovely notion of being an intimate of humanity works only if it is reciprocal—if humanity reveals itself to me."

"Don't they? I mean, humanity has been revealing itself to you—writing you letters and asking you questions in lecture halls—for twenty-five years. And in your experience of life. And now you're answering back."

"Yes, that's true. I'm answering back, in the best way I know how—through writing—in this case, your writing, but my answers. On the other hand, I don't know how much of the private Gene Roddenberry I am ready to reveal. I don't mind telling anyone my *thoughts*—those thoughts that are the products of my logic. My opinions, if they want them, are readily available. My overall dreams for humanity are available to anyone. And I don't mind telling any person whom I would consider a friend my deeper thoughts, provided I think he is ready to hear them. What isn't available are some of the individual impulses and emotions I have. Or my private reasons for those deep thoughts, if they are deep—the kind of reasons we've been discussing off the record. I also have to keep private the opinions I hold of others—the actors, and so on. My evaluation, my word, carries great power in this regard. And I don't want to hurt anyone. And I want to thank you for turning off your recorder at these times. Most people wouldn't do that. They would want to own Gene Roddenberry. I am warmed by that . . . detachment."

"It's on now, you know."

"That's fine. That's okay." He is reflective for a few moments. "On the other hand, I *want* humanity to know *some* of my private motivations—if only to feel that they are entitled to their own. We can decide between us, you and I, which things I am willing to publish now. I want you to remember them all, though. Someday, if you live a great many years longer than I, some of these things may be right to bring forward. In the meantime, we'll just talk."

■　　■　　■

He will be dead in four months. For twice that time, I cannot bear to listen to this tape.

■　　■　　■

"Let's talk about answering those letters," I say. "Assuming most of them are about *Star Trek,* how would you answer them? What would you say?"

"I'd say that I think the best thing that could happen is for *Star Trek* to go off air."

"I don't think Paramount would agree with you on that one."

"No—no, I'm sure they wouldn't. Neither do you, by the look on your face."

"I'm sure you'll explain it in a way that I'll end up agreeing with you, but it's hard to imagine."

"No, I don't think it is, if you think about it," he says. "But I'll explain. *Star Trek* and *Star Trek: The Next Generation* are television shows. They're two different shows, but they are *television shows,* as you are fond of pointing out. When I say *Star Trek,* I'm often not talking about the shows. I'm talking about my dreamworld—my philosophy, the one I wanted to put on television. And I did, to a certain extent. I can't replicate my world on television, because there are too many other considerations involved. It has to make money. It has to comply with current society's standards of decency—of today's values. It can never really fully explore the good side of a supposedly bad thing—and that's what I like to do most. We have to creep around an issue—say, like drugs. We have to condemn them because society condemns them. I'd like our people to go to a planet in which drugs were a way of life—not with all the violence and misery attendant on them now—not as a problem, but a natural part of evolution. A planet, say, where the rain forests have not been raped by the ignorant and the chemicals found in the plants are an enhancement to human consciousness."

"Where, after centuries of ingestion, they become part of the chemical structure of the body and you have a semi-naturally genetically enhanced race?"

"Oh—I hadn't got that far. Yes, that would be a path we could follow—and the things people do differently as a result of that, because they would see things differently. Because of the drugs. Things that perhaps violate our notions of family structure or male and female or even life itself. And the next step up from that plateau—and all the mistakes along the way, all the failures and the triumphs. Oh, no—I couldn't do that now. First of all, you could never do it in a one-hour episode, and second, well, that's the difference between my Star Trek and *Star Trek*, you see. But—and here is the answer—they do converge. They overlap a great deal; they're both times or places, not where there are no problems, but where there are new problems. Or challenges. In both worlds, people are still people, but they have evolved just enough that they don't see color of skin or a belief system when they look at another human being. Or when they look at a person who is not a human being. They see what's inside—the hopes, the fears, the dreams, the struggles—the real person. The way your Little Prince does. They might not like that person—that's their prerogative—but they don't dislike him for such a terrible reason, just because he or she is simply different. They may properly dislike his ideology. They may dislike him because the chemistry between them just works that way. You see the point. They can look at someone and say, 'I don't like him, but I accept his right to live as he chooses. He does things that are not compatible with my way of thinking, but I accept his right to do them. And that may well be because he is from Andromeda or Vulcan, or Russia. It may very well be that there is something about that culture that I don't like. But I won't condemn him. I won't deny him freedom or food or safe passage. I won't deny him his right to worship whatever gods are important to him. I will respect him.' We don't look down on others—as inferior—in the *Star Trek* world, in either *Star Trek* world. We've evolved beyond that. And—"

"Wait—wait, Gene. You're going to have to explain that. This view of tolerance needs to be explored a little more. You're liberal and tolerant about racial equality, abortion, homosexuality, women's rights, sex—all the popular issues—but when you meet up with, say, a Baptist, for example, you will unhesitatingly condemn him to oblivion. You choose your points of tolerance very carefully. It seems to me that when you say you've evolved *beyond* something, that's just another way of saying that whatever you are *beyond*, or think you are, is by definition inferior—that your views are superior."

"Yes, I know. That is a danger," he replies. "It is also an evaluation of progress toward a goal. In, for example the goal of racial equality, I condemn the Ku Klux Klan, for instance. I think my views are superior to theirs."

"Your cat's views are superior to theirs."

"But I wouldn't deny that individuals among them might have other qualities—good qualities. I wouldn't deny them food or housing either, or any other basic human right."

"You mentioned freedom. Is the Ku Klux Klan free to disseminate hatred?"

"Yes. They are, if they are within the law. They are Americans. They have the right to say what they believe, however ignorant or unenlightened they may be. I reject their hatred completely. I oppose them completely. I reject their methods. I reject their reason for having such a cause. They don't even exist in my Star Trek dreamworld. There is no place for them in my philosophy. And my object in the *Star Trek* television show would be to prevent them or stop them and those they speak to from believing it."

"How? These things are learned, as the saying goes, at Mother's knee. Or Father's."

"I don't believe all the things I learned at my mother's knee."

"But you're not the average person."

"Oh," he answers dismissively, "I'm not so different from anyone else. I've had my share of being average. But even if you're right, those thousands of letters you mention are from people who say that they have unlearned some of the prejudices they learned in their childhoods—they have discovered tolerance or the value of peaceful coexistence or the meaning of friendship or this or that from *Star Trek*, some of the very things we are talking about. And as for Baptists, my family was Southern Baptist. I don't condemn them. I don't encourage people to condemn them."

"Well, religion in general, then. I've heard what you had to say about religion—about born-agains and evangelicals in particular. It doesn't sound very tolerant to me."

"Doesn't it? I'm sorry. I never meant to give that impression. If I did, then I will correct it. I condemn charlatans. I condemn false prophets. I condemn the effort to take away the power of rational decision—to drain people of their free will—and a hell of a lot of money in the bargain. And that doesn't just apply to those religions you mentioned. It applies to your religion—and all religions that use the notion of God as a weapon against humanity."

■　　■　　■

The kind of organized religion that infuriated Gene was . . . exploitive. Human beings exploit. Constantly.

—*Robert H. Justman*

. . .

"Religion isn't rational, Gene. That's the basis for faith— the inability to prove anything by rational means. Like the existence of your dreamworld. What if people truly decide to engage in religious practices with the same willing suspension of disbelief as they do when they turn on *Star Trek?* To operate within it for aesthetic, or meditative, or even musical reasons? Or perhaps to incorporate fragments of theology, mythology even, into their lives for their own reasons. Not your reasons. Theirs."

"Do you think evangelists do that?"

"Me? No. I think they're nuts. They make my skin crawl. But I do not claim to be as tolerant as you. And I will go to a traditional Latin Mass, occasionally—for those and other reasons that have *nothing* to do with dogma. Nothing at all."

"Oh, there's no question that the Catholic Church is a very beautiful religion. An art form."

"Well, art may be as akin to beauty, as Keats said beauty was to truth—and therefore part of it."

"Yes, it may be. It very well may be," he says. "But it's not *The* Truth."

"So if religion engenders even *a* truth, how can you dismiss it?"

"Well, first of all, there is a very great difference among these religions you mentioned. There are degrees of idiocy. Some are less culpable than others. But I reject them all, because for most people—not for you, perhaps not for other intelligent people, but for most of these poor devils—it's nothing more than a substitute brain. And a very malfunctioning one. I don't dismiss the people who believe in this or that; I dismiss the structure and, more than that, the very idea of the system of the organized church."

"Then you deprive me of my right to daydream my way through a form of idiocy that I particularly like. You sound as evangelical as your opponents."

"That's a terrible statement to make."

"Give me a reason for retracting it. If you had the power, would you rid the world of churches?"

"Of course not. I would hope that they would go away of their own volition. That people would find it in themselves to write great music and gather and sing and look at lovely pictures and statues and such," he says with a fanciful air. "Or bow and kneel because they felt like it. Or do any of those other things I admire in Catholic and Jewish ceremonies."

"You can't just bow and kneel when you feel like it. It would be a nightmare—everyone popping up and down like groundhogs. It has to be disciplined—choreographed. You might as well go to the set tomorrow and tell Patrick and Michael and Gates—all of them—to sit when they feel like it and speak when they feel like it. Art requires form, structure. You know that."

"I can't believe we're comparing *Star Trek* to a religious ceremony. You're driving me crazy."

.   .   .

. . . *Star Trek* has evolved into a sort of secular parallel to the Catholic Mass. The words of the Mass remain constant, but heaven knows, the music keeps changing . . . religion without theology.

—*Nicholas Meyer, director,*
Star Trek VI: The Undiscovered Country

.   .   .

"If they have nothing else in common," I argue, "they are at least both art forms, and by your own definition, they both exist to convey an ideology, however divergent. It's a valid comparison, for this argument."

"I know it is. That's what's driving me crazy. But in *Star Trek*, we don't tell people *what* to think."

"It doesn't matter, on the premises we are discussing now—art and ideology. That's all we're comparing. How one imparts that ideology is a different argument. But you most certainly do tell people what to think. You tell them to love thy neighbor. You really do, Gene. That's a commandment if I ever heard one. You tell them that violence is wrong, that handicaps are acceptable, that unity is a better goal than divisiveness. All precepts I learned as part of Catholicism."

"No. We point out to them that the consequence of loving thy neighbor is that a more loving world results. They can choose to participate in the creation of that world or not. We tell them that violence breeds violence, and that doing unto others as they would be done by produces very different results. We don't tell them that they must do this or that. And you, in your Catholicism, did what most people do not do— you took the principles to heart and left all the nonsense behind. You're unaffected by that nonsense. Most people aren't so lucky."

"Oh, I'm affected by it—but I understand what it is. I understand the good side of that particular bad thing, if you want to call it that. And I don't think you do—I really don't. Otherwise, you wouldn't be so vehement. Look, all I am saying is that you can't rid the world of something you don't even understand well enough to oppose."

"And all I am saying is that I think your experience of religion is unique. Centuries of misery don't bear you out."

"Do you deny the right of people to choose their own forms of misery? If you want to legalize drugs, you're offering that choice to millions. I mean, why not the opiate of the people as well as the heroin of the people?"

"Choice is the one thing I would never deny to anyone."

"Everyone always has a choice—always. And if they let themselves be persuaded that they do not, then their choice has been to be persuaded. What happens after that is their own responsibility."

"But, you see, that is the very point!" he almost shouts, gesticulating wildly. His fingers are extraordinary—like ten bright, magic wands. "Yes, people always have a choice," he continues. "And they also lack the means to know that they have a choice. I think that, more than anything else, is what I try to convey in these dramas—that they do."

"And if they do not choose what you choose, Gene? What then?"

"Then I congratulate them for having chosen, if it is a real choice, and I wish that their choice may bring them great happiness."

"And you remind them that in the unlikely event that their choice is a bad one, they can always reverse it and maybe then they will be invited to join the Federation?"

"Yes. More or less, yes. And don't look at me like that. This is no different than your university refusing to admit those who are not yet qualified to undertake its work. It's a matter of readiness, not elitism—a matter of choosing a path that leads to something beautiful and meaningful for you—but only if it is a true choice, in which you grow closer to an understanding of yourself."

"So the cathedrals remain standing?"

"Certainly."

"Then I retract my statement."

"But I would discourage humanity from using them for their current purposes. I would discourage, not deny. Yvonne, I must personally condemn a system I see as deserving of condemnation."

"But you don't necessarily condemn the beliefs contained therein?"

"No. Not at all. In *Star Trek*, there is room for many beliefs—and there are many beautiful, helpful values contained in those beliefs. How could I condemn them?"

"By portraying the nature of tolerance as being confined to popular issues. By representing the bad guys as symbols of our current objects of derision: religions, rednecks, conservatives, studio executives, Lawrence Welk, Dan Quayle. I mean, if tolerance is really operative, then you don't dismiss these people as people; you merely question their views. What are you laughing about?"

"Lawrence Welk and Dan Quayle. But of course I don't condemn them—or any of those you mentioned—as human beings. I really don't."

"The test of that is how well you understand them—how well they think you understand them. How you portray them, if you can count any of them among your friends, and how much they count in that humanity you say you love so much. The principle of tolerance is so deeply embedded in you, and therefore in *Star Trek*, that I want to examine it very, very carefully."

"Yes. I count many such people among my friends. Not extremists in any of those categories you mentioned, but some who have a bit of these things in their thinking. Some of them are extremely intelligent people, a few of whom I like very much and with whom I happen to disagree on a number of issues."

"Can you ever say to yourself—or to Spock—that you learn anything from them? Or do you consider the learning to be all on their side?"

"You think I am arrogant?"

"I think you're an enigma: arrogant and humble, a secret supporter of both the sacred and the profane. I know you're trying to take a stand here against what all people of conscience object to—coercion, ignorance, prejudice—but I don't think those vices are the province of one group. There is as much real smugness and real unkindness in liberalism as there is in any other group. I'm not trying to ascertain whether *you* believe in tolerance—I know you do—the whole principle of IDIC[18] emanates from you—but whether your object is also to transcend the self-congratulatory—the very natural pride inherent in believing that one is tolerant, is *beyond* something. It's like taking pride in being humble. And I guess what I'm asking is if humility ever takes precedence in these discussions with ideological opponents."

"You're not going to let me off the hook on this one, are you?"

"I don't think so."

"Okay, to answer your question, no. Humility does not take precedence in these cases. I know what I know—what's right for me. And that's why, in *Star Trek*, we don't go into these issues too much. We let our characters have their own beliefs, without examining them too closely, too often. When we do, I hope it's with some degree of openness, which is what I think you mean by humility in this regard."

"Don't go back to *Star Trek* yet; we're talking about you, personally. What is the use of openness if your mind is already made up?"

"Oh, it isn't. It isn't. My mind is never made up. I'm always hoping to find a new piece of the truth. I change constantly."

"Do you consider it possible that you could find a piece of the truth from someone whom you completely oppose? A

---

[18]IDIC stands for "infinite diversity in infinite combinations," the central principle around which the current *Star Trek* universe is constructed. It is symbolized by a Vulcan ornament that Spock wears, in the episode "Is There in Truth No Beauty?" The IDIC has been made into earrings, rings, and pendants and is worn by many *Star Trek* fans as a tribute to the ideal of universal tolerance for all life-forms.

reactionary? Some lunatic TV evangelist? A racist? How far does your personal tolerance extend?"

"I think it's possible. It wouldn't be one of their fundamental beliefs that I would take as my own, but I might find something in their thinking, something in them, that was better than something that was in me. I would be open to that possibility. What I can say is that I don't think I have ever known a truly despicable human being, although, boy, I've known some that come awfully close. I don't think there is anyone I could 'not love.'"

"Even studio executives?"

"Well, that would take some doing, in many cases, but I'm very serious when I say that if I could look into their lives, into their childhood, and see this influence or that pain, or this disappointment, then I could point out certain things that made them that way. I could give you a reason for the way they are. I *could* understand them."

Who couldn't? I think to myself, but say only, "Can't you assume a reason?"

"Yes, I can. And do, I think, on a large scale. If you look at humanity, their struggles just to grow up—"

"Oh, but I'm not talking about a large scale. It is very easy to be compassionate to humanity. It's far more difficult to be understanding of individuals."

"Yes, it is. I think you may be more compassionate than I. Perhaps it was those years as a nun. Perhaps it's just the way you are. And I don't condemn you to oblivion for your experience as a nun. Far from it. I embrace you, and therefore I embrace it in you. I don't know what the hell I'm embracing. I'm puzzled by it. I'm very puzzled by it—and I don't know how to connect that with you—with our particular intimacy, with your openness. It gives you something that I don't have. And would like to have."

"But then, you have never asked me my reasons for having

been a nun. You may have simply dismissed them as unworthy even of opposition—or thought you knew what they were, which is worse. It never occurred to you, did it, that that very openness could have come from that experience as a nun?"

"Not in a million years. Did it?"

"Largely."

"How?"

I tell him.

"My God," he says when I am finished. "I love knowing that. I really do. Would you like to write something about that for me? With me?"

"Sure. I'd love to. Now tell me why *Star Trek* should go off the air."

He is not listening. "'An incommensurable existence between content and form . . .'" he says to himself. He looks up. "You did say that, didn't you?"

"Among other things."

"Yes, we'll have to write something about that . . . a real socio-organism. . . . You see, I have always tended to look at movements and worry about them. You're right, though. Movements are made up of individuals. But I try. In *Star Trek*, we always try to see the point of even the bad guys. There are no really bad guys. I think you'll find as the series goes on that even the Borg have a redeeming quality or two."

■   ■   ■

An antagonist does not have to be your enemy. That's another thing that Gene was careful to point out to people in his shows. Just because that person—that entity—is your antagonist, doesn't mean that he is bad. It means that he has different needs than you do. . . .

—*Robert H. Justman*

■   ■   ■

"And so why should *Star Trek* go off the air?"

"Well, it shouldn't right now. I think what I said was that the *best* thing that could happen to *Star Trek* would be to go off the air. It isn't, unfortunately, the time for that 'best thing.' That was really only a half-sentence, in order to shock you."

"It did. It would make a great *National Enquirer* headline, wouldn't it? 'Creator of *Star Trek* Hates Own Show.'"

"Yes, they would twist it around into something like that. I despise that kind of journalism."

"People buy it."

"Intelligent people don't buy it."

"And so, with drum roll, what's the other half of the sentence?"

"'Because it's no longer needed.' When it becomes a reality. When we are living it instead of watching it. I'd love that. That would be my dream-come-true."

"And what would the executive producer of *Star Trek* do then?"

"Oh, he'd do something else. He's already thinking of doing something else. I'll tell you all about it at dinner."

■ ■ ■

We dance like this often—on the opposite sides of issues. Another day, we have an almost identical argument in reverse: he embracing my position; I, his. And each of us moves in a number of separate, distinct worlds, few of which know of the existence of the others, none of which overlap, and feel comfortable in separations, divisions, detachments. We feel free.

■ ■ ■

We have forgotten to talk about *Space Cadet,* I remind him as we sit waiting in the hall to go out. Dinner will be at Nicky Blair's that night. It is among his favorite restaurants, full of life and movement, assignations, deals. Predatory women, interested men. Hunger of many kinds. Humanity. The food is excellent. I will wish I am somewhere else. He will talk very little and have an argument with Majel on the way home. When we return, Majel disappears for a few minutes, and Gene says, "I guess you noticed that little disagreement I had with my wife."

I nod.

"I think of her as perfect," he says fiercely. "When I see that she's not, I get angry."

"But Gene, how can you be so stupid?" I start to say, and am suddenly horrified. I am standing in the home of the world-renowned, beloved creator of *Star Trek*, and my host, calling him stupid. I start to apologize.

"Don't," he says. "I *am* stupid about Majel."

·   ·   ·

Later that evening, in an enormous bedroom, which used to be Cary Grant's, I sit looking through my notebooks and thinking. So far, I notice, there are only three real answers to the questions I ask him: humanity, Majel, and Spock. Somehow, these seem to add up to the overall answer, which is *Star Trek*, which in turn is a dreamworld, which, by his own definition, is himself. I am unable to coalesce these streams of consciousness at this point and so turn on the television. It is a documentary about a volcanic eruption. The molten earth pours into the sea. Fire burns on the water. I think of the argument. Water boils on the fire. New ground begins to form. Genesis. A world created by conflict. Water and fire. Pisces and Leo. Volcano. Vulcan. Spock. I go to bed.

·   ·   ·

The next afternoon, I sit on the floor, near Gene's wheelchair, playing with one of the cats. Majel is lying on the couch, intermittently reading, watching a golf tournament, and eating gumdrops. "Have some," she says, throwing some in my direction. "They're really good." A few multicolored Gummi Bears come whizzing across Gene's lap. "Majel, don't throw candy at our friends," he says absently, as one hits me on the cheek.

"They're only two calories," she answers.

I avoid Gene's eyes. When she goes out to the kitchen a minute later to get me some strange papaya to take home, we smile at each other. "I love these absurdities," I tell him.

"Oh, she does it on purpose," he says. "It's wonderful. She keeps the universe straight for me."

I watch him for a few minutes after this exchange. We have no audible conversation. But I know where he is. He is in a new world in which the laws of physics are altered, a world where calories, energy, weight, velocity, mass, force, acceleration, have new, interconnective properties of propulsion, and starships operate on gumdrop principles. The simplest statement from Majel will suddenly fling him into a new universe. I have seen it happen before. I will see it again.

■　　■　　■

One thing we didn't discuss today is how Gene felt about Majel. He loved her. He loved her and he was proud of her. He was so happy with Majel. In his later years, he would just light up when she was around. Majel was a very big part of his life, probably the greatest part of his personal life.

—*Robert H. Justman*

■　　■　　■

He gives me a phone number before I go home, asks me not to give it to anyone else, tells me a time to call him. When I do, he is there, and we go over what I have written. He eliminates one passage, changes his mind about something else. I rewrite it, read it to him, and he is happy. The rest stands. "I'm disturbed about something in my mind," he says.

"What's that?"

"Well, the limits of tolerance. I think I may be more narrow than I would like to be."

"Oh, I don't think so, Gene; it was just a debate. When you meet one of these ideological opponents, you sit and talk and open your heart—you always do, don't you?"

"Yes," he says thoughtfully. "I think I do. I really do."

"It's just a case of hate the sin, love the sinner, whatever you consider that particular sin to be. As you said, there really isn't anyone you could not love."

"Oh, but I might not like them. I might be very happy that I don't have to deal with them."

"Yes, I know. But, as you also say, loving is helping, and maybe the best thing is to help them by not dealing with them—helping them to realize that one of the consequences of their particular beliefs is to be barred from enjoying a friendship with people like you. Or," I add, by this time almost resigned to incorporating *Star Trek* into every conversation, "in the case of the show, from the Federation."

"You are marvelous," he says.

"I am marveling. I'm surprised that it's still bothering you. And I'm sorry. I just want to know what it all means to you— to be so sure of yourself as you always are."

"Not always," he says. "I was not sure of myself—at first," he says haltingly. "I was certain that compared to others, my life was really a small and unimportant thing. As I reached a certain age, I began to think, well maybe not really unimportant, but certainly less important than the rest of the world. And—and it's been a slow rise to accepting the fact that my life is important and is significant and is . . . good."

"When did you start to realize that?"

"It paralleled my success with *Star Trek*—not that because

of *Star Trek*, I was important, but because of *Star Trek*, I had important things to say. I would say the last twelve years, I've been almost certain—no, I've been certain—that my life had meaning. But that certainty, well—it's not always there all of the time."

"What do you most depend on to get you through these times of uncertainty?"

"My imagination. I have lovely evenings with myself in which I dare the world to tell me otherwise."

"You reach reality, then, through imagination? Does something have to go through that process for you, in order to become real?"

"I think so, yes. Nothing is really real to me unless it also exists in my dreamworld."

■   ■   ■

He has a character called Gaan, an alien from an underwater world, who has come to Earth in order to study humanity. He tells me a little about him, and after his death, Majel gives me the treatment for the show that was to have been developed. Gaan, of course, is Gene, I recognize, as I read his observations on humanity. One thing he says reminds me of this conversation: "Until recently, humans have been preoccupied almost exclusively with their external world, believing material things are the only form of reality. The same error characterized their present step into space so far. But fortunately, some of them are at last discovering the existence of inner space. And as they become familiar with inner space, humans will begin to understand, of course, that infinity extends not only outward, but in all directions."

■   ■   ■

In the same conversation, I ask him another question on my list: "What would you not want to lose?"

While he is thinking, I prepare to write down "Spock" or

131

"my imagination" or some equally metaphysical answer. When his answer comes, I am unprepared. "I think I would not like to lose—Ernie," he says.

"Ernie?"

"Yes, my personal assistant. That's right, you haven't met him, have you? He's away on vacation."

"Well, why wouldn't you like to lose Ernie?"

"I think it's because of something I really find I need these days—a kind of forethought, I would say. He is wonderful. He has a way of—he has something that leaves me free . . . to do the things I have to do, and not concern myself with the things I should be doing."

"Why wouldn't you be concerned about the things you should be doing?"

"Oh, I am concerned—but Ernie does them."

"Well, Gene, I hate to say this, but that's one of the chief exercises in a convent or monastery. It's called 'anticipating one's superiors.'"

"I don't consider myself superior to anyone."

"No, and you know I didn't mean that. But as a leader of any large physical and metaphysical concern—someone whose life is made up of a hundred details—the object is to get on with the major concern and not have to deal with all the components. And not have to constantly tell your assistant what to do with each of the details. It means, for the assistant, being astute and sensitive to the needs of the person he is assigned to before those needs arise—to anticipate what it takes to help—to facilitate—a large body of work."

"Oh, yes. That's what I have in Ernie. And he agrees to belong to me for the time that he is with me. I know that I am his job. He is perfect—he understands that. It's a peaceful situation; he leaves me free."

■ ■ ■

Being left "free" is something to which he always returns. He is adamant about freedom. Sometimes it manifests in discussions about intimacy, another subject to which he involuntarily returns often; sometimes he incorporates the notion of freedom into the process of creativity. His greatest battles, both personal and global, have been between the conflicting need for contact and the preservation of freedom, and yet he never seems to come to a conclusion about the correct balance. He will talk about intimacy in terms of being left alone; he will talk about freedom as a vehicle for exploring intimacy; and more often than not, he mentions Hitler.

I learn what he means when he says that he admires Hitler. He does not, of course. What he admires is determination and industry and certain efficiencies that were introduced into Germany during the Third Reich. He admires the fierceness and focus with which an almost impossible task of re-creating something devastated, almost dead, is success-fully executed in the creation of something strong. One of the hallmarks of his thinking is to separate—to see something good embedded in an evil he once said he was happy to fight. He separates the motivation from the result and ends up musing about a system that, if it were not designed to obliterate freedom, would facilitate it beyond imagining. I tell him about monastic life, whose motivation he surprisingly does not reject in this conversation, in which each day is designed to achieve maximum productivity and efficiency, so that one may be left free for study and contemplation and whatever work one has undertaken. He concedes the point. We argue about metaphysics for a moment and return to Ernie.[19] These are the patterns of our conversations—

[19]I had known Gene for several months before meeting his personal assistant, Ernest C. Over. In the last days of Gene's life, no one prolongs it with more care than this tender, faithful man whom Gene does not want to lose.

random links in a chain that will soon connect us irrevoca-
bly. We have one more link to forge. The materials for this
last bright circle are hidden in this phone conversation and
won't be called into use until our next meeting.

■ ■ ■

One day, in the middle of a discussion about "The City on
the Edge of Forever," he decides to explain how airplanes
work, draws pictures in the air with his beautiful hands. His
descriptions are precise and practical. If the nature of humanity eludes him, the principles of aerodynamics do not.
He is a former Pan American World Airways pilot, a bomber
pilot in World War II. I listen carefully, though perplexed by
the abrupt change of subject. When he has finished, I ask him
why the tangent.

"You said last week that you were nervous about air
travel," he reminds me.

"Yes . . ."

"I wanted to help."

■ ■ ■

Undisputably the most popular Original Series episode,
"The City on the Edge of Forever" is a study of help—and a
poignant tribute to the heroic ideal. In this classic tragedy,
Captain Kirk must allow, even facilitate, the death of the
woman he loves (Edith Keeler, played by Joan Collins), in
order to retrieve the destiny of Earth from an alternate
timeline, in which the Nazis were victorious in World War II.
This is one instance when "the needs of the many outweigh
the needs of the few—or the one."

An ironic twist in this striking drama is marked by Kirk's
well-known line, in response to Edith's plea to let her help
him: "Let me help. A hundred years or so from now, I
believe, a famous novelist will write a classic using that

theme. He'll recommend those three words, even over 'I love you.'" Kirk is powerless to help Edith or she, him. Their destinies lie on a grander scale.

He must act out of love, not for her, but for the universe, and she must die to prevent her personal future from destroying the future of all of humanity. It is a story of heroism at its most profound and sacrifice at its highest price.

. . .

I find out later from several of his close friends that Gene himself was very much afraid of flying. I find that impossible to believe. "How can a Pan Am pilot be afraid of flying? How can a U.S. Air Corps bomber pilot sit, as one very old friend put it, terrified in his seat?"

I am sure they are either wrong or joking, until E. Jack Neuman addresses my objections seriously. "Oh, he was never afraid when *he* was flying the plane. Only when someone else was."

. . .

"Helping is loving," Gene says. He goes back to the idea of sexual service for a moment, and then on to a discussion about helping people in the entertainment industry. It is a minor mission of his to launch careers. He keeps an eye out for the promising, the inexperienced but talented, promoting wherever possible, dispensing opportunity. He is proud of the team he says he has put together for *Star Trek*, and says so several times. Toward the end of the discussion, a shift appears. He is now talking about helping *Star Trek*. Always, always the show comes first. He displays that dismissive attitude he so admires in Spock, about even those whom he could help, if they would not contribute to the positive future of his show. We go back to "The City on the Edge of Forever."

"I had a big fight with a writer about that episode. Harlan Ellison. Brilliant writer."

"What were you fighting about?"

"He turned in an episode that was a brilliant piece of work—if there had been no *Star Trek* pattern to follow. And by the time of this episode, we had laid down who our people were—who Scotty was and who the doc was and so on. Harlan treated it as though I had assigned him to do just a science-fiction episode. And I told him that wasn't satisfactory. So, he futzed around with a rewrite. But he just never solved the basic problem of why are we doing this series. Who is Kirk? Who is Spock? And so on. And so I rewrote it. Completely. To the point where he angrily took his name off it."

"So on the credits, does it say 'Written by Gene Roddenberry'?"

"No, it does not. I made a rule that I wouldn't put my name on many episodes, even if I rewrote them entirely, as I so often did. I like to give credit to worthy ideas—to the person who brings them to my attention. It's the fans' favorite episode. And—oh—he didn't pursue that. It was pointed out to him that if he took his name off it, there was no reason that I shouldn't rewrite it if I wanted to and put my name on it. Because clearly, I had changed the whole thing. It really rankled me, because he won the Writers Guild Prize—and I made a complaint about that. I pointed out that if you were to take first drafts and submit them, there are many excellent episodes that could be submitted—but not fairly. Because it doesn't follow the pattern of what you guaranteed to write." In fact, a call to the Writers Guild confirmed that the Writers Guild rule for award consideration, even in the '60s, was that the writer, not the producing company, submitted the script and could submit whatever version he or she chose, be it the writer's first draft or the final shooting script, which usually had undergone many revisions and rewrites by others. Two different panels of judges then made the individual award decisions. That rule is in effect to this day.

"And," Gene continued, "we had a huge fight, and he was as near a thing as I ever had as an enemy. He was a very proud writer. And the very fact that I had rewritten it really upset him. But it was obvious why I had to rewrite it—I had to put our people in."

"I understand that, but it would be hard for any writer. Why not just say, 'No, this is not acceptable. Write something else'?"

"No—because you lose a story then. Why else is this accepted by the fans as one of the best episodes? As the favorite episode?"

"I don't know. It's not mine."

"It's well done, well acted. And I made the studio spend an extra twenty-five thousand on it, in the days when twenty-five thousand isn't what it is today. But there are many shows that I know that, if the first draft were submitted, would win a prize too. In fact, I made the Writers Guild change that rule. For television, it has to be the script that appears on the screen."

■　　■　　■

Gene rewrote everything. But the original writers got the credit.

—*Robert H. Justman*

■　　■　　■

Gene continues. "It was certainly my favorite episode."

"Is it still?"

"Yes. What's yours?"

"'The Empath,' I think. Not sure. Maybe 'Devil in the Dark.'"

137

"Well, it happens to be close to something that is close to you. I love 'The Empath' too. It won an Emmy, you know."

"Yes. And that's odd because it's not a typical episode. But I can't name a favorite. I would give 'moment Emmys' to so many of them. Sometimes, in an average episode, there are spectacular performances, ideas, plots. There are so many scattered throughout the series."

"Well, the object is to get them all in one episode. Or all episodes. You don't look for perfection, then?"

"Not in television."

"Oh," he says. "Well, I do."

"I'm speaking as a viewer now. If I were responsible for creating a show, as you are, I think my answer would be different."

"I'm sure it would. Let me tell you about 'Devil in the Dark.'[20] At the first of *Star Trek*, one of our writers had written an episode that had a planet in it, where miners were mining things, and the writer had created something that I didn't like. It was a story of them discovering large nodules, and in the writer's mind, he would just make them valuable, because they had some chemical composition or something we needed—and that was basically the story. It was basically a story of . . . of . . . ."

"Greed?"

"Greed, yeah. It was Gene Coon who had written that story. And I said, 'Gene, I don't like your story. I'll tell you, it

---

[20]In this study of xenophobia, a group of miners on a planet called Janus VI are being systematically killed by what they perceive as a monster. The *Enterprise* is called in to hunt down the creature, which is a silicon-based life-form that can burrow through stone. Spock, however, joins minds (mind-melds) with the alien, the Horta, and discovers that it is an intelligent life-form, a mother who was killing to protect its children, in the silicon nodules (eggs) the miners were destroying. Kirk negotiates a symbiotic agreement between the Horta and the miners. She and her children will burrow through the mine (they ingest rock for nourishment) and the miners will leave them in peace.

has traces of greed and so on in it, and I would like the story much better if these nodules were created by creatures, and they were eggs.'

"And he said, 'Jesus, Gene—that's a marvelous idea!' Because Gene Coon and I, we thought on the same lines constantly, and that was all part of the *Star Trek* tradition of our attitude toward other races. Up until that time, we hadn't really decided what our point of view on other races would be. And that became so successful—obviously something we had needed to do. It laid out the whole rule of treatment of others. This was really Gene Roddenberry putting together a series—and beginning to state what the series was."

In fact, I find out later that Janos Prohaska, who was a famous stuntman and acrobat, was really responsible for the Horta's egg. Having worked for Bob Justman on the television series *The Outer Limits*, Janos was given the opportunity to create a "creature" for the episode "The Devil in the Dark." As Justman relates:

We made a "spec" deal with Janos. If he came up with a really great creature for a script Gene Coon was writing, we'd rent it and hire him to play the part.

Janos was back within a week's time with his custom-designed creature. It was a large pancake-shaped glob of gook with a thickened raised center and fringe around its circumference. It sure didn't look like much.

As Janos took the glob out of sight to put it on, Gene Coon raised an objection. "Bob, why are we wasting time with this?"

Suddenly, the blob skittered around the corner, making straight for us. Then it stopped, curiously, backed away, and rotated in place. The blob gathered itself up, quivered, made a whimsical up-and-down movement, grunted, and skittered away again—leaving behind a large, round white "egg." Coon was dumbfounded. He had watched the creature giving birth. And, when the creature suddenly turned and scurried back to nuzzle its "child," Gene was sold.

"Great!" he exclaimed. "It's perfect! Just what we need." Then, he excitedly hastened back to his office to finish writing the script.

Gene Coon's "The Devil in the Dark" became one of *Star Trek*'s most famous episodes. And Janos Prohaska played his own creation, one of *Star Trek*'s most famous creatures, the highly imaginative and custom-designed mother Horta.[21]

■　　■　　■

"Yes," I answer Gene, " 'The Devil in the Dark' is a lovely comment about peaceful coexistence between species that could so easily destroy each other. And quite an accurate portrayal of motherhood. I thought it was remarkable."

"Motherhood is important to you."

"As an understatement, that will do."

"Oh, the experience of parenthood is one of the most remarkable experiences," Gene says. "Feelings and instincts arise that . . . that you wouldn't have suspected. I always feel a little sorry for people who don't have the opportunity to be—transformed in this manner. They will always lack a vital human experience."

"And one that cannot be approximated by any other means. It always makes me shudder to hear people say, 'No, I don't have any children, but I have a cat—or a dog.' "

[21]*Inside Star Trek*, by Herbert F. Solow and Robert H. Justman, Pocket Books: New York, 1996, pp. 214–215. There are a good many other memories of Gene's that could have been corrected in this revised edition, but it would be silly to correct them all. I insert this one merely as an example of the fact that although the story did not happen the way Gene told it, the meaning of the episode is not altered by that fact, although I'm happy to be able to give credit where it is due.

"Yes, poor devils." He thinks for a moment. "What an insult to humanity."

■   ■   ■

"I want to say something more about helping," he says. "And I think it will answer some of the other questions I perhaps haven't answered as fully as I could. This is a very personal thing. I have told this story before, but I have a deep personal feeling about this that I'd like to convey now. It changed something inside Gene Roddenberry forever. And it has to do with Arthur C. Clarke."

He leans forward, with his eyes fixed over my shoulder, somewhere in 1969. "When *Star Trek* had its three-year run and was canceled a few weeks before humans landed on the moon," he begins, with a slight irony in his voice, "I was . . . I was—well, I had hoped that *Star Trek* would endure, but there was certainly no certainty that it would. And Arthur C. Clarke, whom I had met and had corresponded with while I was doing *Star Trek*, was lecturing at an astronomy convention. And I made a special trip to hear him and applaud him and see him. And to express my disappointment that we hadn't done anything together before . . . before . . . when *Star Trek* should have been celebrated. And I—I suppose I expressed a little displeasure and disappointment. And Arthur said, 'Oh, my God. I don't think you realize what you've done.' And he proceeded to talk about it in glowing terms, about how I had created something that most intelligent people believed would endure—but I wasn't really convinced. And Arthur said, 'What is your problem?' And I said, 'Well, Arthur, I just would like to be involved in something that is a success.' And he said, 'Well—God—you are a success!' And he said, 'I have a public-speaking company that I am involved in and I'm sure they would love to hear from you.' I pooh-poohed it, but I did go by this company—it was on Fifth Avenue—and the man who was in charge of the company said, 'Arthur Clarke tells me you are a *producer*'—he said it like it was a dirty word." Gene wrinkles his nose and purses his lips as he continues. " 'A televis-i-on pro-doo-cer! And *he* thinks—and I don't know why—that people would *pay money* to hear you comment on your adventures as a television producer.' " Gene does a very funny imitation of this encounter, and we are both laughing as he continues. "Anyway, I signed up, and my first assignment was to go to a small college somewhere in the East—they had room for about four hundred people maximum to sit. And I started to say something to them like 'This doesn't look like a big enough seating area for the people that indicate that they would like to hear me'—and, well, it wasn't. Three thousand people showed up." He shakes his head. "And it went on to be six thousand and ten thousand, and more. I can't tell you what that did for me. You see, Arthur gave me something that I can't even thank him properly for, because nobody—not even he—knew how I felt when *Star Trek* was canceled. I was devastated. And Arthur . . . *helped* me."

■   ■   ■

"A few days ago, in one of my lovely conversations with Spock," he says next, "I came away with a piece of advice. I'd like to pass it on to you—and to anyone who reads this book. He said that one of the great lessons humans have to learn is not to incorporate anything into oneself that will disintegrate one. That is the meaning of integrity—a question you asked me a long time ago. You see how long it takes me to arrive at an answer sometimes? It is a relationship you have with yourself—integration. Integrity. If anything else—any thought or emotion or person—tries to force its way into the space between you and yourself, they've got to go. Without regret, without remorse."

I ask him if he thinks this is consistent with a great love for humanity. He does not even see the connection. "Why would it not be?"

"Because it may do damage to someone else."

"There's nothing damaging about a closed door," he says. "People often damage themselves by beating themselves against it. That human yearning for intimacy carries them into places they have no right to be. It's the product of an adolescent species. They don't understand what it means to be intimate with themselves. How can they truly be intimate with another person? Or people. Spock has a lot to teach us about the maturing of the human race. I'm not responsible— and neither are you, neither is anyone—for anyone else's inability to grow up. We may feel sorry for them, we may try to help them, as far as we can. As far as it is right to do so. But in the end, it is that repeated beating against the door that finally makes people look at themselves. Isn't that something you once said to me?"

"Probably. And intimacy . . . ?" I ask.

". . . comes, I think, only with those who understand that—who have matured enough to understand that—or have not lost the maturity they had as children. That self-contained freedom of childhood. Otherwise, there is always that sense of loss over something that was never theirs in the first place. Great foolishness, and a great waste of time."

∎   ∎   ∎

He treasures the childhood within him—more than any-one realizes, he tells me once, over a single, perfect, glowing glass of wine. Since all of my visits have taken place in such seclusion with him and Majel over many months at this point, this is not a surprise. There is so much evidence of this that it would seem impossible for anyone to think otherwise. He thinks about this for a moment and adds that maybe a few people realize this. When he mentions who these people are,

I am not surprised to hear that except for his wife and mother, they are all writers, all men, and all over sixty, but I am surprised to see, when I meet them, how deeply that understanding is buried beneath a Hollywood persona in one instance, a military brusqueness in another, and an almost frightening intelligence in a third.

Part Three

THE END

▪   ▪   ▪

Gene spends much of his time in a wheelchair now, and
often, when he is getting in or out of it, his shoes fall off. He
wears beautiful shoes—all loafers—and when they slip off,
they are very hard to put back on. One day, I bring him an
ordinary shoehorn, having looked in vain for a more attractive model. His eyes light up. "This is the best present," he
says. "It's the best—because it's thoughtful."

Whenever we go out after that, he shows me the shoehorn.
"I keep it in my pocket all the time," he tells me happily. His
natural, childlike ability to appreciate small wonders, first
evidenced to me by his pleasure in the flower that drifted
onto his head at the Hotel Bel Air, becomes clearer as I spend
more time with him. He likes to be read to as he becomes less
well; likes to hold his friends' hands. He notices colors and
textures with great pleasure. Once, when Ernie wheels him
out to the car, he asks me if I like his shirt. I do. It has purple
stripes and is obviously new. "It's a beautiful shirt," I tell
him, and he is delighted. "It has your favorite color," he
remarks, to my surprise. I don't remember having mentioned
that. And he climbs into his Rolls-Royce, in a thoughtfully

donned shirt, treasuring a cheap plastic shoehorn, and starts to talk about the astrophysical theory of warp drive in the Original Series. I think it is at that moment that I begin to love this frail old man.

His own lovingness, in these last days of his life, becomes apparent. He watches Majel with intense, absorbed pleasure as she moves around the house. "She's beautiful," he says to me once, with spontaneous joy, as if it were a new discovery. He points his finger to a distant part of the garden, where Majel is petting one of the dogs. "Look!" There is an artlessness about him that is more and more evident as he grows frailer.

I buy a strange pair of shoes once—beaded and embroidered with operatic color and form. I show them to him in the box. He lifts them out, turns them over, holds them up to the light, and says, "Magic shoes. How delightful."

"Yes," I say. "All I have to do is click them three times and I'll be back in Kansas."

"Oh, don't do that," he says. "Don't go away."

When he speaks of Spock now, I see that I was wrong. Spock is not an alter ego. He is what adults call "an imaginary friend." Gene just calls him friend. Someone will tell me later that Gene's success lay in the fact that he did— or was—one thing: *Star Trek*. I see that I was wrong in this also, when I took exception to Gene's statement that he was *Star Trek*. That "one thing" calls to mind a Kierkegaardian truth: "Purity of heart is to will one thing." "*Star Trek* is my heart," Gene had said and, in the saying of it, revealed the source of that unclouded vision of childhood he seemed never to have lost. In the vision—or stubbornness—of childhood, he has willed himself into being. He has willed himself to be *Star Trek*. He *is Star Trek*, in his own mind, the same way that Spock is real to him; in the same way as Einstein insists on the supremacy of imagination over knowledge. I think about "I am *Star Trek*," remember that he added "if you see it for what it is." And so I talk to him about its very core, ask him who he is when he says that. I expect him to answer "Spock." He does not. He says, "The Traveler."

. . .

In the first-season episode of *Star Trek: The Next Generation*, "Where No One Has Gone Before," a gentle, intriguing, sensitive alien (the Traveler) comes aboard the *Enterprise* to assist in an engine test. Suddenly, something goes awry. The ship is somewhere where no human has ever been before—a seemingly magical part of the universe where, as the alien explains, time, space, and thought converge. The crew find themselves unable to deal with their own thoughts, which quickly become reality, and are helpless to return the ship to its former position. Having expended his energy during the engine test, the Traveler is weakened to the point of death and cannot muster the force to return them to their own time-space. He tries to explain that controlling one's thoughts, in this dimension, means to control one's reality. Young Wesley Crusher, who has formed a bond with this mysterious being, aids in the Traveler's recovery by the sheer energy of his friendship. As the crew concentrate their thoughts on the Traveler's task, they enable their own return, through him. "Where No One Has Gone Before" is a stunning, evocative episode, full of dreams and questions about the nature of humanity, the power of the mind, and the wonders of the future. This is *Star Trek* at its best:

"Who are you? Or what?"
"I am a traveler."
"A traveler? What is your destination?"
"Destination?"
"Yes. What place are you trying to reach?"
"Ah—place, no—there is no specific place I wish to go."

"Then what is the purpose of your destination?"

"Curiosity."

"That's not an answer."

"I don't know if I can put this in terms you can understand."

"I believe that there may be a warp speed that can get us beyond galaxy M-33, but there is no velocity of any magnitude that can possibly bring us wherever this is. Is it true what our navigational sensors are telling us? Are we millions of light-years away from where we were?"

"Yes."

"Well, what got us here?"

"Thought."

"Thought?"

"You do understand, don't you, that thought is the basis of all reality; the energy of thought, to put it in your terms, is very powerful."

"That's not an explanation."

"I have the ability to act like a lens which focuses thought."

"That's just so much nonsense. You're asking us to believe in magic."

"Well—yes—this could seem like magic to you."

"No—no, it actually makes sense to me. Only the power of thought could explain what has been happening. Especially out here."

"Thought is the essence of where you are now. You do understand the danger, don't you?"

"Chaos. What we think is what happens."

"It pains me I was so careless, Captain. My intent was only to observe, not to cause this. You should not be here until your far, far distant future. Certainly not until you've learned control."

"You are from a different time, aren't you?"

"No—not exactly from another time . . . I—oh, well, as you understand the concept, yes, perhaps that term fits as well as any."

"And you have this ability to travel?"

"Yes."

"And others of your kind have the same ability?"

"Oh, yes."

"Then why, in all our history, has there been no record of you or someone like you ever having visited us?"

"What wonderful arrogance. There has been no record because we have not visited you before."

"Why not?"

"Well, because up until now—if you'll forgive this—you've been . . . uninteresting. It's only now that your life-form merits serious attention. I'm sorry."

■　　■　　■

I talk to Majel about him, his paradoxical juxtaposition of man and child. He really is like that, she says, with tenderness in her face, something very few people see. She looks at me curiously. I tell her about my shoes and Gene and going back to Kansas.

"You're both nuts," she says, and doesn't know why I laugh. Or pretends not to. When I ask her if she's just "keeping the universe straight," she gives me a quick, intelligent smile. "Something like that," she says.

■　　■　　■

I realize what this phrase means the day of the earthquake. We are sitting at breakfast—Gene and Majel in rumpled, matching bathrobes, me in a very old shirt and a pair of jeans outgrown by my son. A few minutes after Majel goes out of the kitchen, the floor begins to shake. Suddenly, there is a loud noise and the chandelier starts swaying. Gene's arms fly out, his hands splayed in a perfect Moro reflex. *"Majel!"* he calls.

We hear a whoop from Majel in the other room. "Well, that was fun, wasn't it?" she says, coming in to give Gene a hug.

"Yes," he says, uncertainly, shakily.

"No," I say flatly, remembering the 1989 quake in the Bay Area.

She reaches out from Gene's arms to give me a pat on the shoulder. "Oh, lighten up," she says, glancing at his face. Later, I find her watching the news anxiously to see if anyone has been hurt.

I read somewhere that Einstein never lost his Moro reflex, and I wonder if it is a characteristic of creativity to retain the instincts of infants, to preserve a certain primate response, which may mean that other, less obvious inheritances of the human condition also remain. I find no information about it, but it is something that keeps coming to mind.

"What is your favorite feeling?" I ask him once on the way to the studio.

"Oh, I love the whole realm of human emotions. I love experiencing them all—even the unpleasant ones. They all have something to teach us."

"Right, but what is your favorite feeling?"

He looks at me sharply, recognizes the repetition as a pattern in his own mind: insistence, consistence, the duel between focus and expansion. A small smile touches his lips. "Pick one?"

"One."

"Longing."

■   ■   ■

There is a glass of water on the table between us, half empty, half full. A football game is on. Ricky the cat sits in the window, feigning disinterest in a flock of birds. We have been speaking of water, toying with the age-old measuring stick of optimism. We are about to speak of relativity.

". . . And so you think the glass is half empty," he says, idly, his eyes on the screen.

"I do."

"Oh," he replies. "I am more of an optimist. I would say the opposite."

"I don't see how that is more optimistic. If the glass began empty, surely it is an optimistic statement to say that it is less so."

"It may be," he answers, and falls silent.

I sense a "but."

"But," he continues, when the commercial comes on, "if I say it is half full, I am indicating its potential to become full."

"And how does what I said deny that?"

"Oh, it doesn't. At least not necessarily. But it might. It depends."

"On?"

"On how one feels about *empty* and *full*."

The cat presses against the window. Gene watches him.

"If the water has been half consumed, then it is diminishing. If it has just been filled to half its capacity, it may be awaiting more liquid. In either case, it is at midpoint, and the same amount of water is present," I tell him.

"That's Spock logic," he says. "Infallible, but not the point."

"What *is* the point?"

"Relativity. One of your favorite subjects. And mine."

The cat makes a lunge for the birds but stops before he hits the window.

"So the question is, to what end is the amount of water relative?"

"That's what I'm trying to get at."

"Well, I don't know, Gene. It would seem to matter how thirsty you were."

"Oh, I'm always thirsty," he says. "I like being thirsty."

■   ■   ■

He keeps himself on the edge of longing, a thin, wavering line between emotion and response, between thought and initiation, between reality and dreams. Longing is what feeds his creativity, he says later—an extended foreplay with the universe, a perpetual mating ritual. He describes it as a terrible hunger. He describes it as an insatiable thirst. I remember a line from a very early *Star Trek* episode called "Charlie X." A young man looks at a woman and says, "When I see you, I feel hungry all over." He is delighted with that line, had forgotten it, repeats it with satisfaction. That's how it is with ideas, he says. Never a woman. The hunger for a female comes very definitely from one part of him, he says. He is in love with the process of longing, with being hungry, thirsty all over, a dance between starvation and satiety. He insists that ideas come to meet him in this dance, that he does not generate them, but only responds to their seduction; that it is not reason that finally hurls him into the creative process, but mutual attraction. He says, "I don't know" so many times that we conclude there can be no more questions. He decides instead to take me somewhere.

"Let's play a game," he suggests. "Shut the door."

When I do so, he closes his eyes. He says nothing. I wait.

"I don't know where you are," I say finally.

"Find me."

I think. Where in all the vast universe of his mind can he be? I think further and come up with nothing. I do not inhabit his world and have no homing instinct. I look for him in a script he had said he was thinking about—in the character of Picard, which formed much of the morning's

152

conversation. Possible planets, issues, ethics, qualities, notions, ideas, and fancies. He seems to be everywhere. It is a clue. He is immensely quiet, but not asleep. This is not the face of the operative subconscious. It is an intensely conscious face. I look around. The painting on the wall seems larger. It is a Michael David Ward print, filled with stars. Finally, I close my eyes. What I say next surprises me. "Warp ten."[22] I open my eyes.

His are still closed. "Why do you say that?" he asks in a perfectly normal voice.

I give the only answer I have: "I don't know."

"Well, then," he replies, opening his eyes and sitting up a little straighter, "*now* is the time to think. That's the place I always start. I start at 'I don't know.' What just happened was not thinking. I do a lot of not thinking. Then when an idea or a person or a picture comes to me, I think about it. Let's think about why you said, 'Warp ten.' "

"Not because of speed," I say. "Theoretically, warping isn't speed."

"No, it's not."

"And warp ten isn't possible, for a spaceship."

---

[22]Warp drive is a delicately balanced, intricate web of chemistry, physics, mathematics, and mystery. Although various crew members seem to understand it, the Traveler in "Where No One Has Gone Before" demonstrates that true understanding of something comes only with the ability to create it. Basically, warp drive involves the bending or "warping" of space, to allow two points to become closer to each other without moving them. Although measured in terms of the speed of light, warp drive has more to do with energy than speed. Nevertheless, the *Star Trek Writers' Technical Manual* establishes that warp factor one is the speed of light, and that *no* ship exceeds warp ten, which is the absolute limit of the universe. In other words, warp ten is the factor at which all points in the universe occupy the same timespace; or, as the manual explains it, "an object at that 'speed' would occupy all points in the universe simultaneously." Factors in warp terminology are "asymptotic," which means that warp factor four is over twice the "speed" of warp factor three. The normal cruising speed of the *Enterprise* in deep space is warp factor six, about three hundred twenty-six times the speed of light.

"I'm not a spaceship. But go on."

"Warp ten is the factor at which all points in the universe occupy the same timespace."

"Is it?"

"I think so."

"Well, never mind," he says. "I'm sure it is, but it's what that represents to you that's important in my mind game."

"It represents timespace. The point of perfect union. I think I was prompted by your painting to look for you in every corner of the cosmos, and I had a fleeting thought—no, impression—that I would need to engage a sort of mental warp ten, as a representative factor, in order to simultaneously look at time and space—that is, the time you might be entering—the future or the past—whatever you were thinking about, and wherever place you were."

"Covering all possibilities," Gene says with approval.

"I guess so. Where were you?"

"It doesn't matter. It's all relative. It was just a way of demonstrating the creative process. You could take that thought you had and turn it into a marvelous story."

"Where were you?"

"Let's try it again. This time, I'll look for you and see what I come up with."

"Where were you?"

"Oh," he says, "where you found me."

■　　■　　■

I think Gene had some kind of Zen going.

—*Robert H. Justman*

■　　■　　■

He was where everybody found him, as he would often say. With a ubiquitous capacity for metamorphosis, a penchant for camouflage, strangely forward and manifestly evasive,

154

neither of which words seemed to mean to him what they meant to anyone else, he took refuge in numbers. *Humanity* instead of *individuals, Star Trek* instead of *me.* We play the game several times during our brief time on Earth together. Each repetition of form produces a different content. It becomes an invaluable source of communication when he is no longer able to hold long verbal conversations. "Find me" is all he needs to say. And there is always something— someone—in him to find.

I have heard it said often that Gene told each person what he or she wanted most to hear. While in some cases that was undoubtedly true, it is an inadequate assessment of his modus operandi, at least at this time of his life. He was one of those people in whose body there lived several others. Confronted with any idea that captured his fancy, he would search his repertoire of internal characters to find one similar to his companion's. If he could find none, then Gene Rodden- berry, whatever that meant, came forcefully into view. We certainly argued enough. And if it were his design to tell me what I wanted to hear, then he failed. I found some of his values appalling, some of his attitudes suspect, some of his personae slightly ridiculous. I would rather not have heard a good many things during that time, and in that house, that I did hear. But I loved the moments of sincerity and simplicity his aged tiredness could not obscure. For in those moments, I saw a Gene Roddenberry that lurked behind the layers many other people called "Gene Roddenberry." Besides, I never knew what I wanted to hear, and therefore, he never knew how to find it.

He tried, sometimes. Succeeded once or twice. Telephoned me in remorse or revision within twenty-four hours of my arriving home in order to discuss it further. The truth is, I never cared about the origin of what he said. Whatever he said was interesting, sincere or not. In one of our strange, synoptic conversations, several weeks before, I had asked him who he would be if he could be someone else for one day.

"It never occurred to me that there *was* anyone else," he answered, laughing, but only half joking.

"Come on. If you had to."

Majel walked in at this point, bearing a plate of peculiar fruit. "Hi."

"Hi. If you weren't yourself, who would you like to be?" I asked.

"Um . . . if I weren't myself, who would I like to be?"

"Yes."

"Here—have some of this. You've never had it before." She offered a dish of yellow cubes that looked remarkably like those rubbery food squares the crew ate in the first season of *Star Trek*.

"How do you know I've never had it before?" I asked.

"Because you haven't. It doesn't grow anywhere else. It's a strange form of papaya that sort of drops off the trees up there on the hill."

I think how appropriate and ironic it is that something grows on Roddenberry land that grows nowhere else, while she considers the question.

"If I weren't me, who would I like to be? Nobody. I can't think of anyone I'd like to be."

"Well, just for a day, then. One day."

"I'd like to be a movie star—but that would have to be *me* who was it, not somebody else. No—there's no one."

I can't believe that anyone would deny himself or herself that experience. Gene and Majel read my face and laugh.

"I told her the same thing," Gene says to Majel. "Odd that we both had the same answer."

They look at each other and laugh again, as if at some private joke, and Majel walks down the hall.

´ "I can't imagine that anyone would pass up that experience," I tell him.

"Oh, you would make an excellent casting suggestion."

"What?"

"A casting suggestion. You probably think more like an actress than Majel does."

"I am an actress," I say. "I just don't act in movies—I act in real life."

"Well, that's exactly why I said I don't need to be anyone else for a day. I already am. Despite what I have said about actors and actresses, that was a compliment I gave you, you know."

"No, I didn't. But thank you. And why?"

"Because I think it is very important to enter into experiences as if you were part of them. To become other people, to act out different roles. I've always done that. And it has always served me well."

"But you wouldn't call yourself an actor."

"I think I just have. All the world's a stage, isn't it?"

"Is that dishonest, do you think?"

"No. Everybody acts. The dishonesty of people is in not admitting it. How else do you learn to be a baseball player, an airline pilot, a friend? You act as though you were. You take on the properties of whatever that role or that relationship requires. And you become so. Or you don't—if it doesn't work out. I am a very different person in private than I am in public. That's a simplistic division—it's just one of many. As you know."

"No, I don't know. I've never seen you in public."

"No—that's right, you haven't, have you? And so—good. You are not blinded by that."

"Might I be blinded by that very fact? If your public self is just as real?"

"No, I don't think so. My public self is real. But it is a

reality I have created. My private self is—is just what you see. I may choose to be my public self in a private situation—with someone I don't know well. I'm still Gene Roddenberry, but I don't present all of Gene Roddenberry to everyone. Or anyone. I don't even know if I could: I'm still exploring myself—I'm still finding out some things I can be. It's the human adventure. That's why children play. That's why adults change jobs or relationships, or take up new interests: to explore the vast possibilities of who they are. I *am* the things I try to be, while I am trying. And if it works out, fine. Then that new thing becomes a part of me. I think you're disturbed over a word you're probably going to bring up next—*sincerity*."

"I was going to say *authenticity*."

"Okay, let's talk about that."

"You talk. I'll listen."

■   ■   ■

Gene made his way—and he had many different careers. But his best career and his biggest career was that of human being. He was the most human of human beings. I loved him.

—*Robert H. Justman*

■   ■   ■

"I think the core of who a person is remains steady," Gene says thoughtfully. "If you are a shy person, then you'll be a shy cop, a shy airline pilot, a shy writer. You might hide that shyness—you may even overcome it—but you carry the shyness and the ability to overcome it into your various roles. If you're an intellectual, you'll always think that way. It will be of service to you in some situations and not in others. There are times when it might do you harm. But you'll still have that way of thinking, that way of looking at life, in whatever you do. People judge other people on such superficial ground that they are very quick to call someone a hypocrite when they come up against a side of them they hadn't seen before or are not equipped to deal with. I've been called a hypocrite on flimsier ground than even that—because I saw two sides of an issue when someone wanted me to see one."

"It is said that the mark of a genius is to hold two opposing opinions at the same time," I say.

"Then I must be the smartest man that ever lived. I hold dozens of opinions on dozens of issues all the time," he says with a laugh.

"And so when you are called a hypocrite, what do you do?"

"Do? Nothing, of course."

"What if it is someone—a friend—whose goodwill you covet, whose respect you would like to keep?"

"I think you can be pretty sure that if someone seriously calls you a hypocrite, then he or she is not a friend. Besides, that rarely happens. There are so few people who know more than three or four compatible sides of me, at most."

"Rarely. But it does. Has."

"Yes. Well, then, I am sorry for their limitations, and I go my way and they go theirs."

"Does that bother you?"

"No."

"Does it bother them?"

"Probably. I'll tell you something that bothers me. Now that I have achieved some measure of success, certain people allow from me what they would never accept from others. Because I am Gene Roddenberry. That's hypocritical. Oh, they may spar with me a little bit—a little bit—they're very careful not to do it too much. But they do not allow others the same freedom with them. I mean, who the fuck is Gene Roddenberry? He's a guy. If I weren't famous, I'd still be that same guy, maybe sitting next to them in a bar. We'd strike up a conversation, and I would express the same opinions, and guess what? I'd get punched in the nose."

"So—Gene, how do you reconcile all your selves?"

"Oh, I don't. I know who I am. How do you?"

"Same answer. It just doesn't bother me."

"That would be the rest of my answer too," he says. "It just doesn't bother me."

"But it might bother others."

"Well, then, you just have to say what I say in those instances."

"What?"

"Fuck 'em."

■   ■   ■

We are, of course, speaking on different levels here, although I did not realize it at the time. I am using the word *act* in its literal and classic sense: "to do, to drive, to conduct." I am saying that I act or accomplish things in the roles of mother, university instructor, writer, et cetera, appropriate to the situation. In each of these roles, my values, opinions, character, remain the same. Gene is saying that to act is to pretend, and sometimes the pretense ends up being real— that to one person, he will espouse views that to another person he would deny. He sees nothing wrong with this. I do.

■   ■   ■

"Tell me about success," I say.

"What about it?"

"Do you think success emasculates one in some way?"

"No. The opposite."

"Opposite?"

"Yes."

"How?" I ask.

"Success is a process of seeking answers for yourself. Every

160

time you seek an answer and find an answer, you grow a little further. There's nothing in the seeking of answers and the finding of answers that diminishes you. Because when you find an answer and then later find out it is a wrong answer, you are persuaded that there are other things that you don't know. And it does not in any way diminish you. All it does is rule out certain things that in your past foolishness you thought were right but were wrong. And therefore that gives you the direction to seek further."

"Yes," I say, "that's internal success. But as far as external success goes, often when people become more successful, they become less human. Less—nice."

"Well, that is a judgment they make on the world."

"They make?"

"Yes, they become less nice, some of them, because they have decided that niceness will really fuck you up—stand in your way of really achieving other successes too."

"Do you think that's true?"

"For some people in some ways—not for me, because I adjust to that."

"You mean you're just as nice as you used to be?"

"Oh, yeah—nicer."

"Why nicer?"

"Well, for one thing, the longer I live, the more I discover about humanity's weaknesses—and learn to forgive. I understand why they are weak. I learn to understand it. Oh, I am so much a nicer person than I was as a young man. How can I be anything other—when I see the foolishness of people for almost seventy years—and learn from the foolishness of people and not be a better person, having learned from those things?"

"Well, by becoming bitter. People often get frustrated when they see the foolishness of others, as you call it."

"Oh, then they're not reading it properly. What would

bitterness be in that case? That there are things that force us in the way we don't want to go? Bullshit! That person is not reading the lessons of life properly. I don't promise you that every decision I make will be a right decision, but I do promise you that every decision I make will be more right than past decisions! And there may be a great gap there, between the correct decisions—but I'm inching up. And that's why I say that I am a much more pleasant person than I was."

"Do you think everyone else will say that about you too?"

"No. Some persons have been attracted to false paths."

■　　■　　■

Success may emasculate you if you let success go to your head. It emasculates you of your morality. That can happen if you're not a strong person. And sad to say, most people aren't that strong. People allow success to turn them. They start believing that they are as intelligent and as omnipotent as their newfound "friends" tell them they are. Success didn't emasculate Gene.

—*Robert H. Justman*

■　　■　　■

"Yes, but you know," I argue, "people who have been successful in whatever they do often end up with a lot of . . . stuff. Material wealth. And servants and so on. Which make life easier. And then they become less tolerant of anything that is not what they want to do, when they want to do it. Or having what they want, when they want it. You can see it. It shows on their faces. That self-absorption. How does that improve the inner man?"

"You think that you drive down a typical street in a typical middle-class neighborhood and you don't see the same faces?"

"I don't know. I live in an affluent neighborhood. I'm concerned sometimes about what I see."

"I think I do know. And I will tell you. I think in the best of all possible worlds—in the world I dream of, in *Star Trek*—it is a better world because it is a wealthier world. You don't have any needs to drive you into bitterness. There's plenty of food. What one is concerned with is not food and physical success; one is concerned with happiness. And there is less and less unhappiness in the world that I visualize. Because it's a wealthier world. You don't have these things. You don't have people saying, 'God—it's terrible, because I've never had a chance, you know—I've never really had a chance.' And, oh boy—that can create terrible bitterness. You don't have these people in the *Star Trek* world I dream about. You don't have people chasing unrealized dreams, and that's what makes you bitter and disappointed and makes you choose false dreams. In the *Star Trek* future, people don't choose false dreams because the whole canopy of excitement and self-realization is always there."

■　　■　　■

He is not addressing current reality, something I have come to expect. To him, there is no point in looking at a problem in one time dimension. He believes in the future. It is here, adjacent to—or perhaps intrinsic to—the present. It is his extraordinary ability to ignore time that gives rise to his views, and his ability to convince others of that fact that gives rise to change.

■　　■　　■

"There is no money in *Star Trek*," I remark. "Money doesn't even exist."

"No. Money is a terrible thing. Why do people work at jobs in *Star Trek*? Why does someone become a baker? Because the family is going to starve to death? No. People become bakers because certain people love the smell of things baking and certain people take pride—we all have a little pride—in something. 'Let me give this to you because it's delicious and you will love it.'"

"'And I made it.'"

"'And I made it, yes! And this is my recipe.'" He looks into his mind for a moment. "All things will be taken care of."

He has an odd way of speaking today: like a prophet, a parent, and a cosmic administrator all at the same time.

"For example, I was looking for someone's father," he says, not bothering to tell me he was looking in his head. He knows I know, by this time. "And he was a very wise man and he had spent much of his life out in space, contemplating these things. And what this father had decided to do was adopt a square mile of forest and work in that square mile—and make it better. And fertilize things and prune saplings and make everything in that square mile the best possible thing. God, that would be . . . wouldn't that be a wonderful way to live?" He looks at me with shining eyes.

"Yes, especially if you were feeling it all the time."

"Well, you probably would if it were a thing you wanted to feel. So you see, the need to work should not be a financial need, particularly when we are part of a better world. It is true. I haven't worked for money in the last twenty years. I've done good work because it's necessary for me to do good work—my . . . my pride—I couldn't write a bad script if I tried. I have to write good scripts because I like things working out properly. And I happen to be one who likes scripts to be lovely and pleasant and spell a little message that says to you and my son and a thousand other people, 'It's best that you do something good.' And that's my way, and it pays rich dividends, but never a dividend that I have worked for."

"No," I say, feeling a sudden surge of affection for this

simple, complex, happily contradictory man. "No, you have to do what you love."

■   ■   ■

"So what do you think of me so far?" He leans back and smiles.

"That you are a very religious person," I say, to see what will happen.

His face is worth a thousand words. "You can't possibly think that."

"Oh, but I do."

He thinks of arguing. I can see it rise in his face. He changes his mind. "Why?" he asks, very politely.

"Will you accept the definition of religion simply as ideology, just for the moment?"

"Only because I love you."

"Then I think that you are immersed in an ideology called *Star Trek*; that you adhere or try to adhere to its precepts, even as they change, or you change them; that its epistemology is enlightenment, or evolution if you prefer; and that you have your own personal Trinity: Humanity, Wife, and Holy Spirit."

"Who's the Holy Spirit?" he asks.

I give him a look.

"Spock," we both say together.

"I dislike the word *holy*," he says, "but there is a certain attitude I have toward Spock; I hold him in a kind of awe. His intelligence, his mastery over the problem-solving process. I think I would disagree with your terms, if only because they represent historical definitions, but I can accept their meaning. You may well be right. I don't know. I'll have to think about that one. Spock has for me so much significance—such personal and impersonal appeal. My Spock, not the one you see in *Star Trek*, although they are similar."

165

"What's the impersonal appeal?"

"Just that. Impersonal."

"I don't understand."

"Well, I don't know that I do either. It's a way he has of being detached but not deficient. He has a coldness to him that I admire."

"Why do you admire coldness?"

"Perhaps that's a bad description. I mean he has the ability to focus on a thing with such intensity that he freezes out distractions. But he remains intact. Spock is an intact entity. He dismisses extraneous concerns when he is involved in problem solving. He removes himself and even his great intellect, so that his inner wisdom takes over. He can belong to the present moment, in a way that I never can. Majel has that ability. She can focus. She lives entirely in the present. It's a great asset, at times. A great asset. I don't know what it is about Spock that enables him to do that so well. It's something I have to make an effort to achieve."

"Maybe he is more limited than you. You always see so many sides of everything."

"Maybe. Maybe, too, he has that ability you have of cutting through the crap. I don't know. I call it a kind of coldness. I love it. It leaves me free. A very positive trait."

■   ■   ■

Within a few months, both Majel and I will have each been called cold. I note the circumstances, remember this conversation, do not mention it, and take the accusation as a compliment. Majel ignores it. Once it has been said, the present is past. She has no interest in it.

■   ■   ■

"I think it's bizarre that we let religions prepare our answers for us rather than use our brains," Gene continues. "Think how much less Spock and Kirk and Picard and all of them would be if they debated answers from the viewpoint of religion. It is impossible to conceive of these people having secret guidance from something outside themselves."

"Well, Spock does, in a certain way."

"What?"

"Spock. He has meditations, and he has guidance from the whole of Vulcan, as is demonstrated in more than one episode—and implied at least in the films. Look at the end of *Star Trek III: The Search for Spock*."

"He has guidance from all he has perceived in the universe, from what seem to be answers that are suggested to him, but these are not religious answers."

"No, but they are from a source outside himself. He's in touch with something other than his own particular unit of being; he's in touch with the thoughts of other Vulcans, apparently. Isn't he?"

"No."

"Let's put it this way: he certainly has times when he reflects on a number of issues in meditation."

"Well," Gene says reluctantly, "he reflects on all these things, and questions them in his mind and so on, yes, but I don't think he seeks answers. There's a difference between searching for answers from out of his own experience and seeking answers magically."

"I'm not talking about magic—or answers; I'm talking about ethics."

"Oh." Gene laughs, and then looks puzzled. "Oh. Well, then, I don't know."

■　　■　　■

"You know what I think?" I say to Gene, one morning at breakfast.

"No," he says. "But I'm always glad to find out."

"Well, something that Isaac Asimov created in *The Naked Sun*. About viewing versus seeing."

"Refresh my memory."

"The people called Solarians, one of the fifty outerworlds that humans had colonized many years before, created a culture in which they were entirely dependent on robots, and their estates were so large that they rarely had contact with anyone—neighbors, friends. Eventually, they evolved a culture in which each adult lived alone, surrounded by robots, and communicated with others only by viewing—a kind of holographic visiting, called trimensional viewing."

"Oh, yes," he says. "I may have borrowed that holographic idea from Isaac; I don't remember."

"Well, even though this holograph was a simultaneous, present transmission—that is, not a tape—they never considered themselves to be 'seen' by another person. So if they were having a bath or doing any other private activity—not sex, because they couldn't stand human contact—they would visit with you via holograph. But they would never dream of being seen in that state. They felt that the projection of themselves was not the same as themselves. And I wonder, sometimes, if that isn't what you do. You project yourself, and it is yourself, but, well, it's not the same as really seeing you."

"Well, but you would only know that because you see me. If you didn't, you wouldn't know the difference."

"Is there a difference?"

"Of course."

"So . . ."

"So those who can, see. Those who can't, view."

■　　■　　■

"I'm sorry that I have never had a homosexual relationship," he remarks pensively, out of the blue, one afternoon, "because I know that there must be many joys and pleasures and degrees of closeness in those relationships. I think that I have in a way been cursed by having picked my particular time period and background and so on, because I have no doubt that I am capable of homosexualism."

"Do you think everyone is? Bisexual, I mean?"

"Oh, yes. But you are a piece of your particular world and the different strengths of emotions that formed you and so on. The things you were taught to regard as correct. But I am very pleased with the fact that I have come out of that way of thinking, in my time . . . as a matter of fact, remind me. I'm in the midst of making a decision about homosexuality— male and female—and how we are going to treat it on *Star Trek*, the lovely ways in which we will treat it—without defying present average conventions."

"Remind you what?"

"To mention that I am presently thinking very deeply about that."

By this, I assume that this will be subject for a later conversation. It never is. His hour of death is approaching.

■   ■   ■

I am interested in the fact that he said he picked his time and place, as if he remembered an existence before existence. When I ask him if he believes in reincarnation, he says no. He amends this statement later, asks me to substitute the words *I don't know*. I think back to a conversation we had once when he was very tired. To hear the voice that speaks from its electronic repository now is to hear something hovering in the back of the primal consciousness, prophetic and haunting. Some of his friends insist that he did not know he was dying. He did.

"What defeats you?" I had asked him in a previous conversation. It was just next on the list of questions and had no particular significance until he answered it.

"I think the same thing that defeats you from time to time.

You just can't . . . stay ahead of . . . humanity. You can't stay ahead of these characters." His voice, which would be strong the next day, was fragile, ephemeral, old. "You just . . ." He pauses for a long time. ". . . You have to occasionally say, 'I give up on that. . . . I need a . . . I need to *rest*. I need to rethink the universe for a while.' And—and then I think that having acknowledged the fact that you're human, and a part of all this, the fact *it* has the knowledge that does defeat you from time to time, then God, or whatever it is, somehow allows you to back up. Maybe take a fresh run at it. I—I'm just defeated by the fact that there are not enough thoughts in this vessel to really work it all out."

.   .   .

I wish I had learned more of humankind, of your own concept of your creator. I have seen much to criticize in mankind. But I believe there's even more to admire. Had I more time, I might have learned to understand humanity's greatest of all achievements: the ability to feel love for one another.

—*Questor*, The Questor Tapes

.   .   .

We speak of love once. It arises out of silence one morning when he is not feeling well. He is tired. His eyes register pain. I stop asking questions, and by unspoken agreement, we sit in his study, wordless: I, on the floor, writing, he dozing lightly in his chair. Once or twice, he looks down with an apologetic smile. When I have finished my notes, he is deeply asleep. I rest my head on the arm of his chair, and later awake to find his hand tapping my cheek.

"I'm feeling better," he says politely and untruthfully. "What shall we talk about?"

THE END

I look up into a face from which the life is draining daily, and can think of only one thing. "How about love?"

"Sounds good," he replies. "I'll just collect my thoughts. What do you think about it?"

"I think that you do not want to be loved."

"That's nonsense," he says, startled and somewhat pleased at this new challenge. "What makes you say that?"

"It's true, isn't it?"

"Of course it's not true. I *love* love."

"But you love loving. You don't much care for being loved."

"I don't see how you can say that," he answers, with a laugh. "You know me better than that."

While I am thinking of how to explain what I mean, he frowns. "You're not giving me that 'fear of intimacy' shit, are you? Because if you are, I've heard it before."

"No. I'm giving you some Saint Francis shit."

"Saint Francis? Now what are you talking about?" He sits up straighter, ready for battle.

"Your approach to life, your philosophy, remind me of Saint Francis of Assisi."

His face is a perfect portrait of consternation. "I never know what you're going to say next," he says. "How can I remind you of a saint, in the first place? And, in the second place, you may know me, but you don't know what he was really like. Or," he adds with a laugh, "do you?"

"Sort of. I was a Franciscan."

"Oh, well," he says, thinking this one over. "Well, well, go on."

"There is a prayer, call it a yearning, attributed to Saint Francis. I'll say it to you. Just to avoid argument, I'll leave out the references to the disputed deity, and while I'm saying it, you think of Starfleet, Captain Kirk, the Prime Directive, and Gene Roddenberry, okay?"

"Okay," he says, settling back and preparing to be amused.

I begin. As I recite it, his face changes. His thumb begins to rotate.

> *Make me an instrument of peace.*
> *Where there is hatred, let me sow love;*
> *Where there is injury, pardon;*
> *Where there is doubt, faith;*
> *Where there is despair, hope;*
> *Where there is darkness, light;*
> *And where there is sadness, joy.*
> *Grant that I may not so much seek*
> *To be consoled as to console;*
> *To be understood as to understand;*
> *To be loved, as to love.*

"There's more," I tell him, "but that's the relevant part."

He lets out a long breath, says nothing for a time. Finally, he shakes his head slowly. "That's very beautiful," he says in a quiet voice. "Is that how you think of me—an instrument of peace?"

"I think a lot of people think of you—and *Star Trek*—like that."

"Oh, I would love that. I hope I am, in some small way, an instrument of peace." He sighs, reaches down, and kisses the top of my head. "I'm so happy to know you," he says.

"And, you see, the part about being loved, Gene—just from knowing you these few months, it seems to me that it is a matter of focus. Your purpose, or mission, or job—you say it yourself—is to love humanity. Being loved is secondary. At least, being loved in the traditional sense. It strikes me that you love humanity not because it is made up of individuals whom you cherish, but, rather, you love individuals because they are representatives of humanity, the whole socio-organism. And so, love in its ordinary one-on-one manifesta-

172

tion, in which you love and are loved, just isn't that important. Maybe because being an instrument of peace is more important. Helping people love each other."

"I never would have thought about it like that," he says, "but I have to say you're right." He looks at me strangely. "How do you know this?"

"I don't know that I do. It's just a thought."

"Well, with that thought, I think you have hit the core of Gene Roddenberry. And *Star Trek*, as you said. I really do. I'm going to do some pretty hard thinking about it. We weren't really playing our game, but this time, you found me." He shakes his head again. "You found me, all right."

■   ■   ■

We return to the subject of controversial topics for *Star Trek*.

"You see," he says, "writing is really at the heart of it all. Everything depends on a good script. Some of the things we were talking about are awaiting a good script. Of course they're awaiting something even more important, and that is a certain readiness on the part of the audience. I have to be careful, not so much with what I decide to put on a particular show, but how I treat it. I could do a show about homosexuality, for example, and have half the viewers cheering me on. Well, in the case of our audience, not half. I hope we have a greater percentage of enlightenment than that, in our fans. But to do a pro-gay episode—or any other controversial issue—you have to do this." He holds up his thumb and finger spaced about a half inch apart.

"A little at a time?"

"A little at a time. People have to get used to these things. They have to get used to a certain liberation of thought, in the same manner as captive animals need to get used to freedom when you let them out of their cages. Suddenly they've got to survive in a world of options. Nobody's going to feed

them. Nobody's going to tell them that this or that option is
bad or good. They'll have to try different things and see if
something works. And if it doesn't, what should they do
next? Oh, yes—a whole world opens up."

"Meanwhile dealing with all the others who have opted
not to leave the cage," I say. "Don't forget them. The peer-
pressure lot."

"Oh, the first duty is to get away from them as soon as
possible. You can come back later, when you've gained a little
confidence and maturity and say, 'Look here, this is what I've
found.' I think the best stories in drama have been about this
kind of unappreciated enlightenment. But let's look at these
few adventurers who've gone into strange new worlds. They
have their own cage philosophy inside them; they've got to
fight that too. Humans are so wonderful, so brave. It's
astonishing, the way the human spirit has survived. There
are so many shows I would like to create based on variations
of this theme."

"But you're not still actively engaged in producing *Next
Gen.*"

"Not as active as I once was. My people are all good
people—Rick Berman in particular. I trust him to produce
my show. And he does. But I still look at everything. I make
my evaluations and put my stamp of approval on everything.
Nothing goes on that I don't approve."

I have seen some of this, of course. In the many weeks of
our unfolding communication, we have gone over scripts
together, watched dailies together, discussed the relative
merits of one word over another in line changes. He has sent
me over to the set of *Star Trek VI: The Undiscovered Country*,
where I have watched the legendary Kirk and Spock in
action. We have discussed that legend and how it affected the
production of *The Next Generation*, and I have heard him on
the phone with a great number of staff with regard to the

show. Watching dailies is so different from watching the finished product that a thought arises.

"Do you ever watch *Star Trek* on TV?" I ask.

"Oh, yes. Sometimes with a sense of wonder." He shakes his head in obvious delight. "It's twenty-five years old!" he says, as if it were a new thought, and is clearly in awe of his own creation.

"I'd like to watch it with you," I tell him. "It would be like a triple time shift—creator and created; progenitor and descendant; subject, object, and observer. *Star Trek* or *Next Gen*—or both."

"Let's do that," he says enthusiastically. "I'd like to do that. Yes, and we can comment."

∎ ∎ ∎

We do. But we do not comment. It is weeks later. He is in the hospital. They have attached him to wires, bored holes in his head. Injected, medicated, monitored him. Now they come in to test him. A team of doctors ask him questions to determine the state of his—logical capacity, memory, brain functions? I don't know. They ask him the date, the year, to count this and answer that. He makes a few mistakes. When they leave, he says to me, "Time?" I say, "A couple of minutes after seven." He looks at the television in his room and says, "*Star Trek*." I turn it on. The *Enterprise* sails across the screen. Whatever else he forgets in the last days of his life, this is not one. Nor is his critical ability impaired in that world. Once, one of the characters says something he does not like. "No," he says. I do not speak. He is working.

∎ ∎ ∎

He wants to talk about actors now, the medium of his dream: what they represent, how they convey meaning, what happens to the written word when it becomes the spoken, the difference between good acting and good performance. Three-dimensional entertainment. He asks me so many questions that it is difficult to ask my own. When I do, he replies candidly, then asks me not to repeat most of it. I erase the tape, make a few notes, and ask his permission to include the following. He agrees.

"I want to tell you something," he says, conspiratorially. "I share something very fundamental with actors."

"Oh?"

"Yes. It's a kind of belief. When they get up there and pretend to be—or take on—a certain character, they have such a belief, the good ones, that that character exists. I'm like that. I like to believe in that, and I'm amazed that it still happens, because I created all this—and I see what's behind it all—and it still works. I can be moved, like the audience. I love that."

"You can still be the audience?"

"Oh, yes. Isn't it wonderful? I'm still a viewer. And as a viewer yourself," he says, leaning forward with interest, "tell me what good acting means to you."

"I suppose when the actor disappears and the character takes over."

"Yes, I think that's largely true. It's a noble ideal, but then of course when they achieve it, they complain that they're typecast and wallow in misery about it." He searches his conscience for a moment. "Some of them," he adds.

I ask him who. He tells me. We go on.

"Who disappears to you in *Star Trek?*" he asks.

"Oh, Leonard, of course. He really becomes Spock."

Gene starts to speak. I interrupt him. "I know you are Spock, but you aren't the manifestation of Spock. Leonard's face, his fingers, the way he breathes in, in distress—that is the corporeal Spock. Leonard does tend to disappear. Ask anyone to show you a picture of Spock; they'll show you Leonard Nimoy's face."

He is quiet for a while. "He really did do a wonderful job, didn't he?" he says in final acknowledgment. "I was—I am—very proud of him. I wonder how much of the internal Spock he has left in him."

.　　.　　.

When I meet Leonard Nimoy a few months later, I search for signs of Spock in his face. They are there. Whatever else is there, he keeps hidden. He will not talk to me.

.　　.　　.

"Who else?" Gene asks, coming back from a personal trip into the past. "Who else disappears?"

"Oh, all of them, I suppose. Leonard, consistently. Patrick Stewart, certainly. I don't know. I am the worst person to judge."

"Surely not. One of the best, I would say."

"But I'm not a representative viewer," I tell him. "I often watch television and movies for very bad reasons. Or rather very good reasons of my own. Bad as a judge for your purposes. I'm really not qualified to answer that question."

He, of course, becomes more interested. "Tell me anyway."

"Okay. We're going to have an argument, I can tell, but to me, the words often mean more than anything. Not just their meaning, although that is most important, but their sound. I would watch *Star Trek* if Patrick Stewart read all the parts. Or Brent. Or any of the principals, really, to see what shape they took, what meaning they had, when coming out of different mouths."

"Oh, yes," he says, "but you wouldn't watch it every week. After that particular approach had been explored—and it might be a very interesting thing to explore—you'd look for something else. You'd return to our format, because it is more complex, and that is what makes it consistently interesting."

"No doubt. But I think it's amazing how form changes

content, depending on the actor. When you find one whose suspension of self allows the script to come through, for that particular character, then you watch it for the acting as well as the words."

"So far I can't argue with that. Would you like to be a casting director?"

"No. Because to me, if you have a really good script—as you consistently do in *Next Gen*—then I'd watch it. Whether anyone disappeared or not. The script takes over sometimes."

"Bad acting can ruin a script. People won't watch that."

"I will."

He shakes his head. "No, you wouldn't."

"I told you: I'm the wrong person to ask."

"Perhaps you shouldn't be a casting director."

"Oh, I *know* if it's good acting or not. I just don't care sometimes. It's the words, you see."

"What do you mean?" Gene says. "Words speak louder than acting?"

"Yes, sometimes they do. When they are saying something. At other times, they don't matter at all."

"When don't they?" Gene asks, genuinely puzzled.

"Oh, well, for that matter, if it were announced that Charlton Heston were going to recite his grocery list on television at six o'clock this evening, I'd tape it."

Gene leans back and roars with laughter. "Heston? Oh, you wouldn't have to do that. He's a friend of Majel's. She can call him up and maybe he'll come down and read our grocery list to you." He chuckles. "I'm dying to know your reasons for this one."

I look at him.

"I'm serious. I really am," he says. "We may be getting to some fundamental ideas about acting that I want to explore."

"Oh, it has very little to do with acting. It might be the flick of an eyelid, a cheekbone, a mesmerizing inflection, the ability to cry copiously and silently, with grace. Bits. Not the whole performance. I might watch a movie for two hours to see someone blow out a match. As far as Mr. Heston goes, I *can't* know if he is a good actor or not. He is bound up with a transitional moment in my life—he is a ten-year-old's version of the heroic ideal versus the fallible and the inevitable. I thought he was *the* perfect actor then. I preserve that in myself; I refuse to judge. No, I would listen to the grocery list because of the perfect moment—the second, the nanosecond—in which, perhaps, *A sack of dog food,* because of the timbre of his voice, becomes present. The dog food is there. I see it."

"And you don't think that is good acting?" Gene smiles.

"It is a good performance. It is a miraculous performance if the dog food materializes—spills from its blue sack on the wet tile floor."

"You're talking about radio, not television."

"No, I'm not."

"Well . . ." He struggles between objection and curiosity. Curiosity wins. "What if it doesn't?"

"Doesn't what?"

"Doesn't materialize—you don't *see* the dog food."

"Oh, then I just trip out on his nose. He has a perfect nose."

"Somehow, I don't think that means what it would mean if someone else said it. Why don't you tell me a little more about it."

"No. You're supposed to be doing the talking."

"Oh, I'll have plenty to say in a minute. You go on."

"Well," I reply, "that's exactly why I *am* talking about television. I think actors—or to be precise, visible actors— are . . . are objects, in a sense. They have—or should have— no substance of their own. No content. They should be conduits of content—of the script—they should disappear.

Their characters should inhabit them. But if they don't, or don't entirely, or don't always, then one can invest them with one's own content, or they can provide simple visual pleasure. They can be a springboard for—I don't know—musing, perhaps. Heston's nose in that case takes on the same meaning as a Caravaggio—a Vermeer nose. It becomes representational. We move—I move—from the expectation of infusion to one of perception. He—all actors—are like paintings or sculptures. It is up to them to become their own Pygmalions and burst into life. And if, for some reason, they don't or can't, then there is always the delightful possibility of the principle of Heston's nose. Representational reality."

"I've always said that television is art. I absolutely agree with you on that. And it goes back to one of the earliest principles of theater. Greek theater set out to achieve that interrelationship between the visual and verbal. It's a very pure form of entertainment, isn't it? Very sparse and beautiful."

"Oh, yes. People wailing in tragedy with grapes hanging off their heads."

He laughs again. "So you invest a performance with your own imagination?"

"If it allows that."

"You might like to be a producer. A producer has a very special relationship with the audience. He has to see a performance from both sides of the screen, something a writer can't always do. We get marvelous scripts sometimes, but they just won't work for television. I'm always sorry about that."

"Can't you make them work?"

"Not usually, in those instances. Usually, we just have to take the idea and dispense with some very wonderful writing that would be better off in a book. We talked about that Harlan Ellison script. That's something I've learned from experience. I've never found out why. I just know it. It's just television. I want to go back to your caveat."

"What do you mean?"

"You said you often watch something for bad reasons—or good reasons of your own. When you watch something at other times, for its own merits as a production, what sorts of things would they be?"

"Talking heads. *Masterpiece Theatre* sometimes. *Star Trek* and *Next Gen, The Roadrunner* . . ."

"The cartoon?"

"Yes."

"Why?"

"Timing, I think. It's a masterpiece of timing. The roadrunner always says, 'Beep, beep' about two seconds after you expect him to. It's great comedy. Or at least I think it's funny."

"Oh, yes. Timing is very important. In humor and in drama. How interesting. What else?"

"Mostly British productions. In fact, probably ninety-five percent. Almost any play or any adaptation of a nineteenth-century or other classic novel. No offense, but I think in general, British TV is superior to American TV. *Sherlock Holmes*, with Jeremy Brett, or *I, Claudius*, for example. We have our counterparts, of course. *Roots* is one; there are others. Most of what I watch is PBS stuff. But I also watch American TV—actually, reruns sometimes. I don't have a lot of time, but when I do, I watch *Dragnet* because—I don't know why, really. It's campy."

"I used to write for *Dragnet*. How lovely to hear that you watch it."

"Yes, I know. It reminds me of *Star Trek*, the Original Series, sometimes."

"In what way?"

"It has a similar earnestness. Its comments on society are

almost a plea to humanity. I don't know—maybe it's all that orange paint and plastic plants. I don't have a profound reason. I just like it. Recognizing it for what it is. It's not Tennessee Williams. Why are you asking all the questions?"

"I'm coming to a point. Now tell me what it is in all that mix of very different productions you mentioned that motivates you to turn on the television—to watch something for its wholeness rather than its parts. And afterward, to say, 'That was a good show.' Or even 'a great show'?"

"Forgetfulness."

"What?"

"I forget that I am there. I forget to think my thoughts. I think the thoughts of those characters on the screen. I guess I forget that I am a separate person. I guess it all adds up to representation of self. I am no longer an observer; I am those characters—they are me."

"Yes. Character. Exactly. And that is art. In *Star Trek*, we try not just to make you see the dog food—although that is a wonderful thing, a wonderful thing to be able to do, especially for an audience such as you, who would want to create images of her own—but in *Star Trek*, we want you to be the one reciting that list of groceries, to see how it feels to say, 'A box of dog food' yourself. And that's why I say television is art. Some people may think that is a silly thing to say, but I believe it."

"Why?"

Gene shifts painfully in his chair. He is tiring earlier these days. "I'll tell you why in a minute," he says. "But first, let me tell you why I disagree with you, on two points you made. First of all, an actor has to keep some of his own content—he really does. That's what makes one actor different from another. Maybe what you mean is that he has to get rid of a certain amount of ego, in the Jungian sense. In most cases, a great amount of ego."

"Actually, I didn't mean that. I meant what I said. So you can feel quite comfortable in denouncing it. And anyway, I know you're going to make me change my mind. Besides, you're the producer of the most beloved, most watched show on television. I really have no right to disagree with you on this subject at all."

"Oh no, no, no. I am the producer of the most watched and most beloved show on television for only one reason. Because there's an audience out there; there are fans. I try to tell my people this constantly—the actors especially. God, I wish it wasn't so hard to get this through their heads. They can turn out the most magnificent performance ever filmed, and if there's no one there, it means nothing. Drama is storytelling, communicating between people. If there is no audience to communicate with, there is no show. Period. We owe our existence to the viewers."

"You also owe your existence to the production. If there is no show, or if it is an inadequate show, there is no audience."

"Yes, of course, that's a given. I am so convinced of the excellence of our series that I wouldn't think to mention that. But it's a symbiotic relationship. And that means that there is equal value in each. Equal. You must respect the audience. Many of them are more intelligent than the actors and actresses they watch. Try to tell an actor or actress that. But anyway, my point is that you have every right to discuss your experience as a viewer with any producer in the world—and not just you, but anyone. In fact, I would call it an obligation. There would be a lot less crap on American television today if more producers spent more time talking with the people they're trying to reach. A lot less crap.

"In our show, well, our fans feel rather proprietary about it. More the first show than our current series. As they should. They saved it, in the third season. And still today, they feel an obligation to respond to what we put out there in front of them every week. And that's good. That's a wonderful thing. I don't let the fans run my show. I run my show. But, boy, do I listen. And I'm really not disagreeing with you, personally. You have very—unique—reasons for the way you perceive things. But an average television audience doesn't look at a show in this poetic way, so let me address you now as that representative audience you spoke of.

"Going back to that ego thing, I think you were closer to the truth when you said, 'a suspension of self.' An actor has to suspend his or her ego in order to let the character get through, not obliterate himself. It's an intermix—*suspension* is a good word. A really good actor coexists with his character; he has a personal relationship with him, and he bows out graciously to let the character shine. Actors have to feel what the character feels—I'm sure this isn't news to you—but they have to keep just enough ego to turn in a real, human, believable performance. They can't be watching themselves act, like so many bad actors do. In that sense, they have to disappear, yes. I think I agreed with you on that. But they have to disappear to themselves, not to the audience. Not completely, or else it's no different from having robots playing the part of humans."

"That would be interesting. I'd love to see that."

"Oh, no. That would be . . . that would be . . . It *would* be interesting, wouldn't it?" He stops for a moment, riveted by this idea. "Maybe that's the way it is in the future, and actors are those who control the robots' movements and program their voices."

"Yes, a thespian renaissance. A company of Datas, doing Shakespeare. Except that Data is an android, not a robot, as he's always saying. What's the difference anyway?"

He is still contemplating mechanical actors brought to life by their human counterparts, in some distant segment of time. "What?" he asks. "Oh—I don't know, exactly. I don't remember. Actually I do know, but I've forgotten for the moment. You might ask Brent tomorrow. I'm taking you to the studio. I want you to spend time on the set and see for yourself what it takes to bring my *Star Trek* to life." He returns to the idea of robots. "There is a technology out there that is working on that very possibility."

We get sidetracked on what is now called virtual reality. When that discussion ends, I have to play back the tape to find out where we were.

"You said you disagreed with me on two points," I say. "What's the second?"

"Oh—the reference to Pygmalion, that actors should become their own Pygmalions, bring themselves to life. That is true, but it's a role they share with the director. A good director gets into the characters—from a different standpoint. He draws out that life. You'll see that tomorrow. And I think that largely happens on our show. We have excellent directors; all our people are first class. And now I'm going to tell you a little secret: I *like* our people."

"That's no secret."

"Oh, it is," he says, "because some folks out there may think that I have said it in the past to be supportive or to convey some wonderful impression. The secret part is that it's the truth. I want you to say that for me. This is strictly 'for the record.' I'm genuinely very happy with the cast we have now. And I think that they are happy with each other."

■　　■　　■

He goes on to tell me various stories about the strengths, weaknesses, vulnerabilities, talents he has observed in each of "his people." He discusses their early interviews, their development into the characters they portray, his perception of them as people and as performers. It is strictly off the record, but when he concludes, I ask permission to quote his last sentence. He gives it: "They are all beloved to me."

■　　■　　■

When we are discussing the former conversation—editing specific examples, deleting extraneous asides—we begin to talk about acting again. Something immediately comes to mind that I am hesitant to say.

"Go on, say it," Gene says. "I think I know what you're thinking."

"Well, *Star Trek* (the Original Series) . . ."

"What about it?"

"Look, I love the show. That's why I'm here—I found something interesting in it that prompted me to go to the source of all those ideas. But . . ."

"It isn't always well acted? Is that what you're so reluctant to say? Don't be. It isn't going to hurt my feelings."

"Well, that's the problem. But that's also the point. It just doesn't matter. And in fact, I think if it had been more polished, more subtle, then it wouldn't have had the impact it did."

"Well, now why would you say that? There is so much I would improve on if I were doing it again. Not just acting, but—oh, so many things. As I have done in *The Next Generation*. You're not speaking of that series, are you?"

"No," I answer him. "I think what I mean is that the Original Series was more representational—more like classic mythology—with an idealism expressed in a representative way. Kirk, hero, period. Spock, logic, period. Like Superman or Flash Gordon or Roy Rogers. You look at them—I look at them—more as figures of qualities, courage, compassion, et cetera. Personifications of the ideal."

"Like Greek theater?"

"Maybe. Maybe that's why I love it. Or maybe it's that Heston thing. I refuse to judge. And please don't think I am disparaging the cast, because I'm not. I don't think that an Academy Award performance is the point."

"Emmy," he says. "It's a television show. But all right, that may be part of the reason it had and continues to have such appeal. Perhaps the acting suits the purpose in a way you don't realize. Because you come away with a perfect sense of character, don't you? You know who Kirk is and Uhura and all of them. You could tell me right now what Sulu would do and what he wouldn't. You have a sense of them as people."

"Absolutely. Perhaps it is perfect acting. I don't know. I know that I watch it, even though it's not *Masterpiece Theatre* or *Roots*. I know that I feel great affection for the characters. They are who they are completely, but they're not really anybody I might meet on the street."

"No, but they might be people you might like to meet on the street. I think I understand you, but I would take exception to your notion that acting consists only of the kinds of performances given in those two examples you mention. Other kinds of acting are just as valid. I think that's your problem. You're looking for a kind of great drama in a television show that was designed to sell a product—to keep many millions of people buying that product. PBS shows don't have to do that. And, as I told you, I am thinking of doing a series that could easily fit that bill. But I understand, and I think we have come to a different way of expressing ideas in *The Next Generation*. It is more subtle, as you point out. We have more money and more time and more freedom to create something that is more of what we expect today. We don't need to hammer people over the head with messages. They're there, all right, but I think we get them across in much better ways—we incorporate more qualities within each character—so that you don't have Picard, hero, period. They all have their heroic qualities and their failings. They are all less of a caricature of a particular quality. And they all have room to improve, in a believable, down-to-earth way. So much of my philosophy hinges on improvement, on evolution. We continue to evolve in the *Star Trek* world."

"I don't want to go on record as saying that the acting is bad in *Star Trek*. I don't mean that."

"It's your book. You don't have to go on record as saying anything you don't want to."

"But this is an important point. That show is unprecedented in the history of television. It has spawned a subculture that is rapidly becoming part of mainstream culture. With its weird sets and rubbery aliens and a sort of larger-than-life method of acting, why does it survive?"

"It survives, I think, because it fills a need," he says slowly. "We need that larger-than-life experience. You see, you wouldn't love it if the acting wasn't exactly what it is—an identification with these very strong characters. And if the characters were larger than life, then that's what they had to do—show that."

"Yes, and it was twenty-five years ago: all television was different—younger—then. Which is why, I guess, you often refer to the two *Star Trek* shows as 'the growing up of Gene Roddenberry.' I'm not questioning why we loved it then. It's more a question of why it is equally or even more beloved now, in the '90s. Even though *Next Gen* is so extraordinarily successful, people still watch the Original Series."

"Possibly because it is the '90s. This isn't a very happy time for humanity. And in *Star Trek*, both of them, my dreams speak to the inner wish of humanity to be happy, to live in a world where such people might exist. People of courage, people who can disagree with one another and not let their disagreements erupt into war, who can simply say, 'I will not interfere with your way of life—and thank you for not interfering with mine.' To be a part of the *Star Trek* dream means to be the sort of person who does not have to depend on others for self-worth or self-definition, who has been given the chance by the very world he is living in to seek his own answers. Not to be afraid of that. And the original cast got that message across very well—boy, did they get that message across. And continue to."

■   ■   ■

I am curious about why he wanted to spend so much time talking about acting. His answer to that is that television is dangerous. "It is the most dangerous force in the world today."

Literate humans have known for dozens of centuries that people's opinions and values are affected by what they see, and that dramatic portrayals of life are often much stronger than the reality around people. . . . This is what literature is all about, whether it is carried in the printed word or on stage or in a comic book or on an electric tube. Drama, and particularly fictional drama, has always had enormous effects on the audience, much more than facts or news usually do, because the essence of drama is to take the audience and force them to become part of the story, to identify with the participants, and to feel as they feel, and often to think as they think. So there is no question that what people see on television affects them, but this very fact opens up a whole spectrum of subjects that are usually ignored. . . . For example, did the juvenile commit violence because he saw a similar version portrayed on the screen, or was it because his attitudes and values had already been twisted and eroded by all of the television he had been watching for years? This is where the simplistic cause-and-effect arguments break down. How could you blame a robbery dramatization on one show and ignore the damage caused by years of anesthetizing the juvenile's brain

189

with inane kiddie shows, the vulgar materialism of game shows, where he is seeing adults prostituting themselves into jackasses to win a new car, and the snake-oil commercials, in which even a child can see the inherent deceit?

—Congressional Record *statement of Gene Roddenberry*

■　　■　　■

"You see," he says, "I would really prefer to do a show that would not have to rely on advertising to appear on television. I'd like to do a series along the lines that you mentioned— that would have a much smaller audience. But that would be irresponsible of me, because I have ideas that I know are right for our time, and they have to reach the greatest number of people possible. And that, for now, means commercial television. It is a restriction, but it is one I willingly accept because of the benefits. I may lose something as a creator, as a writer, but it is nothing compared to what millions would lose if we didn't have a *Star Trek* to dream about."

There is a look on his face that I have come to recognize: it is remote, determined, austere. A Spock look.

"There is a future," he says, with the emphasis on *is*, "and it is because of people like Kirk and Picard and so on— people who recognize that the future is a personal responsibility."

"Like you?"

"Yes. I have to do what I can. And television is the way I can do it. That's why the actors and the acting are so important. Don't mistake me—it is a team effort; no one is more important than anyone else. The supervising producers, the editors, the makeup—I want you to see everything— special effects, wardrobe, everything. We'll do that. I want you to be part of this. And when you've seen everything, I want you to tell me—from everything we've said, everything we've talked about—how much you see of my Star Trek dreamworld in my *Star Trek* television show. But—and here's a big but—the actors are what the public sees. When Picard makes a wonderful, thrilling statement, the audience will say, 'Picard is a man who believes in this or that. Isn't he marvelous? Isn't he intelligent?' And maybe, 'I would like to be like that.' And they start thinking like that. And they begin to . . . to . . .''

"Embody some of the traits of the future?"

"Yes, exactly. The kind of future we need. They don't say, 'Wow, isn't that writer John Doe fabulous? What wonderful things he dreams of—I would like to be like that.' Oh, no—it is the actors who carry the message. It's not fair, but that's the way it is. And that's why I try to choose people to whom this is not just a job. It's not always possible, but I think everyone feels, in different degrees, that what we are doing is valuable, that it means something."

"You wrote the guidelines for every character and every creature of the Original Series, is that right?"

"Yeah," he says, adding with a laugh, "although I didn't know that that wasn't what I was supposed to be doing in addition to everything else."

"Whose job is that, normally?"

"That's usually a writer who has had some experience in creating series," he says. "Which I wasn't. But I just assumed that if you're going to create a series, you create the whole idea for the series—and so it went for five years, at the end of which time I thought I was Mr. Star Trek."

"Weren't you?"

"No." He slowly switches gears from writer to producer. "As years went by, the studio said—what can you expect?— 'Here's this guy—what are his credits?' If it hadn't been for plain stubbornness, I probably would have given up. But I refused to accept the fact that I was a Johnny-come-lately who perhaps had had a clever idea and was hanging on to that idea tenaciously. The end of that part of the story is that [by the time of *Star Trek: The Next Generation*] literally dozens of people had tried to redo *Star Trek*. They saw no reason not to bring in a proper writer who understood how this thing should be done—and indeed they did, but none of the things were any good. I refused to cooperate with anything but my own show, and I refused to even listen to anyone—these guys who they had tried to get to rewrite *Star Trek*—it was obvious to me that this wasn't the way to go. There's only one way to do *Star Trek*: the way I want it. I've spent a lot of time fighting off people who want to *fix Star Trek*."

"Really? I find that very odd."

"It doesn't happen with *Star Trek: The Next Generation*. They do it the way I want it."

I object. "Well, you know, it's not *just* the way you want it. It has to be that they [the studio] want it the way you want it, or it just wouldn't work."

"That's right. It hasn't worked for many of the movies."

"Which ones?"

"Five," he says firmly. "Two," he adds in a loud voice.[23]

"Two? But it's a very clever story."

"But it's not *Star Trek*," he says stubbornly. "Four was *Star Trek*."

■ ■ ■

He suddenly launches into a discussion about Leonard Nimoy and William Shatner. It appears to be a puzzle to him as to why there is an estrangement between them and *Star Trek*, meaning himself.

---

[23]Five refers to *Star Trek: The Final Frontier*, the fifth *Star Trek* film, and *two* refers to *Star Trek: The Wrath of Khan*, the second *Star Trek* film. *Four* refers to *Star Trek: The Voyage Home*, the fourth *Star Trek* film.

THE END

". . . The others have always been loyal to me, loyal to *Star Trek*," he continues. "Nichelle is wonderful. George and Jimmy and Walter—they're wonderful. I want you to meet them. You will find a very special quality in those people."

"You left out DeForest Kelley."

"Oh—I didn't mean to. De's a friend. I would say a real one. Forgive me, De! You see, that's why I didn't like most of the movies. I wanted the other characters to be brought back strongly; I wanted to create what we finally created in Four (*Star Trek IV: The Voyage Home*). The secondary actors remained loyal to me, loyal to the *Star Trek* ideal. I don't know what Six will be like. If I like it, I'll put my name on it. If I don't, I won't."

"May I quote you on this?"

"No. I don't want to hurt anyone. Write it up and read it to me on the phone. I'll let you know."

■　　■　　■

Above is the edited result. (I have been asked to offer some additional insight on this conflict, which Gene talked about at length, but I won't. It's old, it's tired, and it matters only to the people involved. It's their right to tell the story—if they want to.)

"So you see," he goes on, "actors and acting are crucial to my purpose."

"The actors are helping to create a future, your vision of the future, by representing it on television. By making the present, future—and the future, present."

"Yes. If there were another, better way to do it, I would. I prefer books. In fact, I am writing a book right now. It's about what happens to Kirk after he retires from Starfleet. Who is he then? What does he become? But books just don't have the impact they used to, which I think is unfortunate. But I work with these misfortunes. I do what I have to."

"What is it, in one sentence, that you have to do? What is your Prime Directive?"

"In one sentence? Ensure that when the future arrives, there are still humans in it."

■   ■   ■

We who are in the television industry and take our responsibilities seriously often do not know whether to laugh or cry when family-hour censorship comes up, because it is censorship that created this unwanted violence everyone is talking about. We in the industry are not that barren of ideas . . . we are capable of fashioning an exciting drama out of the thousands of real issues of life and the rights and wrongs of conflicts which exist in everything: sex, religion, politics, corporate life, militarism, and everything else. The structure of television, however, does not allow our people often to write on these things, and when you take all the meaningful subjects away from a writer, all you have left is sex and violence with which to provide the conflict that is necessary to draw the mass audience. This is not because television networks are evil, or that their executives are thoughtless men. Like us, they work in a medium whose primary corporate purpose is really not to entertain, and not to inform, and this is something that is very seldom brought up when these subjects come up. Our basic problem is this is not the primary purpose of television. The primary purpose of television is to sell products. It is structured that way, not because of any diabolical plan, but because that is the way it happened to grow up. And these commercial messages demand mass audiences, and often this means the lower and lower-middle bulk audiences, whose opinions are sufficiently malleable to be changed by commercial messages. I think, even more unfortunately, it is these same malleable minds which are most likely to be convinced that the meaning of life, the alpha and omega of existence, is in that breathtaking vista somewhere between *The Beverly Hillbillies* and *Let's Make a Deal.* We are no longer dealing with that pleasant little idiot-box gadget which we can watch occasionally for entertainment and some shopping information. We are dealing in television, gentlemen, with a sound and image device of incredible potency, which is now being used in this country at the astonishing rate of something like billions of people-hours each week. It begins to appear that our children are watching television for two hours for every one hour actually spent studying or reading books. And the adults probably come off with much less. And to make this picture worse, our most respected engineers and scientists in this field tell us that the telecommunications explosion is really just beginning. What we are probably dealing with now, gentlemen, is nothing less than a wholly new form of human communications, and it is something that may be as significant in its own way, if you can believe this, as the invention of the Gutenberg press, but we have no guarantee that the results of this are going to be anywhere nearly as happy.

—Congressional Record *statement of Gene Roddenberry*

■   ■   ■

"So you see," he says simply, "I have to make *Star Trek*. I just have to."

■   ■   ■

"Gene," I say one evening under the stars, "what is it that makes you love humanity? Is it initiation or response?"

"What?"

"Well, so many people love you, or think they do, or love parts of you, or love what you do, which is part of you, then it would make it difficult for you not to respond similarly."

"Yes, but . . . I felt that way before it was a response."

We are quiet for a while.

"My mother tells a story," he says, "about dreaming of what she would do for all of her friends if she could. It was a wish, and it was to give all her friends gifts of the things they wanted most to have. I've heard that story several times, and I think it was something I was born with because of her."

"Have you been happy most of your life?"

"Yes. More the last part of my life. This is why I scolded you a little bit about people who have success—that it makes them worse people, because that is generally not true. The more success a person has, the better the hopes for that person."

"That's what Somerset Maugham says—that the idea that success spoils people by making them vain, egotistic, and self-complacent is wrong. It is failure that makes people bitter and cruel."

"Well, that must be why I loved Maugham from the first."

"And Mom," I say, wondering when I will meet her.

"And Mom," Gene says, smiling.

■   ■   ■

When I meet his mother, I feel a sense of recognition in this gentle, fragile lady. She is almost broken with grief over the death of her son, but speaks of him tearlessly. In the many visits and talks I have with her, she tells me stories and incidents of Gene's life. One thing brings him sharply to mind and gives a reason for her quiet tearless sorrow: "I think of him all the time," she says. "I daydream about him."

■   ■   ■

THE END

"The point of the writer," Somerset Maugham says, in *The Summing Up*, "is that he is not one man, but many. It is because he is many that he can create many, and the measure of his greatness is the number of selves that he comprises. . . . His daydreams are so significant to him that it is the world of sense that is shadowy, and he has to reach out for it with an effort of will. His castles in Spain are no baseless fabric, but real castles that he lives in."

When I read that passage, in the process of confirming the other one, the last link in the chain of our conversations forms, meets the first, clicks shut.

■   ■   ■

"Do you remember," I ask Gene, "what you said on the phone a while back—about your imagination, about nothing being real unless it exists in your dreamworld?"

"Yes, but not exactly. Play it back for me."

"I can't play it back. We were on the phone; I didn't tape it. But I wrote it down." I read it to him.

"'. . . Nothing is really real to me unless it also exists in my dreamworld.'"

"Oh, yes," he says. "That's generally true. Why do you ask?"

"Majel."

"Oh," he says, looking toward the house. We are in the garden. It is colder now.

"You 'daydream about her.' She is 'part of your dreamworld.' You get 'angry when she is not perfect.' She 'keeps the universe straight' for you. She was your 'best friend,' but now Spock is, and yet you often speak of her as having the qualities Spock has: focus, living in the present, a kind of intimate detachment. And you say you can't get into her dreamworld."

He looks around as though for a means of escape. His

thumb begins its customary cycle. "Well?" he asks after a moment.

"Well, but that is what you want, isn't it? Your favorite feeling is longing. You love longing—for the future, for elusive dreams, for answers, for her. That's where it all comes from, isn't it—this world you've created? It comes from longing, from not entirely possessing anything. Which, by the way, has a great deal in common with the monastic ideal. But that aside, there isn't really anything you want to . . . to have. Possess. Own. You just want it to be there, close enough so that you can long for it, far enough away that you can never reach it. And that's why reality doesn't really count unless it makes that leap fully, into your head—where you can re-create it."

He says nothing.

"She's a real person, Gene. You didn't create her. You asked me to explain her. I can't. All I know is that if you want to, you have to confront the living animal, not just a portrait mounted on the wall of your dreams. And if you think you can't get into her dreamworld, I'm surprised. You spend most of your life in it: her dreamworld is you."

He looks angry for a moment and turns his face from me.

"I'm sorry if this is intrusive—I really am," I tell him, "but I didn't ask for this—this—assignment. You gave it to me. And that's my answer, for all it's worth."

He is silent for a long time.

"Give me a hug," he says finally, with his face still turned. When I do, he buries his face in my side.

"God, I love her," he says.

■　　■　　■

He seems to believe in perfection. He has to. It is what he shares with those religions of the world he so despises and the philosophers he has studied with meticulous care. It is what he admires in his fictional heroes, what he created a hunger for in millions who watch *Star Trek,* what propels him toward the future. Perfection is what he says he seeks, not only for humanity, but for himself. And while he can excuse any amount of foolishness and fault in the whole of humanity, he cannot bear it within himself, when he recognizes it. Or whatever exists inside himself. I think back to that senseless statement I wrote in my notebook. "If Gene is *Star Trek,* then Majel is Gene." Other fragments of memory flood in to surround those words: that near absence of ego— of selfhood—I detected in Majel so long ago, her seemingly irrelevant statement about cutting the ribbon so it fits. The way she has of looking like she is inhabiting her body temporarily, as if her real existence lay somewhere else. That sacrificial "greater love than this has no one" guillotine posture, that conviction that he is, if not perfect, at least a personal ideal. Somehow in the process of incorporating her into his dreamworld, he became hers. Metaphysically, she has little existence outside of him. And when he confronts what is left, he does not recognize it. It isn't perfect. Somehow, they have become dreams to each other.

I think of Spock, how hard it is for Gene to accept Leonard Nimoy in that role. And yet Leonard's book, *I Am Not Spock,* shows elements of the same self-identification, evidence of the same incarnation, echoes of the same conversations. Creator and created battle in a timeless repetition of Caliban and Setebos, in an effort to wrest existence out of a dream. The closer one is to him, the greater expectation he has, and no one is closer to him than Majel and Spock. In the eighteen months that follow his death, I talk to his friends. Of the few he calls intimate friends (all male), all of them see this conundrum. Of the females, none do. He has been, if not deceptive about his inner self, at least fiercely protective. He has thrown up a smoke screen, which at times has been interpreted by others, and seemed to say: Majel is not perfect; therefore, she does not exist. When, in the last, revealing days of his life, he opens a final door, the smoke clears. He looks at her, a few weeks before he dies, and never takes his eyes from her again.

. . .

It could all be nonsense of course, I think, as I write the passage above. But it isn't. I know why it isn't, but I can say no more. There are enough books out there spilling secrets and blood. No more is necessary, for above this labyrinth of intimacy that lies too deep for tears or answers, they are strangely connected people—separate, together, quarrelsome, peaceful, alive. It is only the extension of their contorted passion into the *Star Trek* world that makes it significant to any except themselves. *Star Trek* exists because of both of them.

. . .

I remember a conversation we had about his son. At the time a vital, electrically energetic seventeen-year-old with a fierce intelligence and dreams of his own, Rod was another source of perfection in his father's eyes. It was during a conversation on anger that the subject came up. "What makes you angry?" I had asked him, and he said, "Nothing." After arguing about that answer for a few minutes, I said, in exasperation, "Well, you have a son. Doesn't he ever make you angry?"

"Oh *no*," Gene says with an unusual vigor. "Of course not. I love him. How could he make me angry? He's perfect." Without accepting this answer, I grow to understand what he means. It is the Rod in his head with whom he is never angry. Happily, in this instance, the real Rod approximates the dream boy. There is intense connection between them, and less definition of what perfection means in a son. For Gene, it is enough that Rod exists, in both worlds. The joy of that existence keeps him from what he defines as anger. But anger changes definition throughout our conversations. It is a feeling, like fear, that is often cast aside for greater purposes—like the need to create the world of *Star Trek*, in which there is little to be angry about. Later, he admits that as a father, his children sometimes make him "damned annoyed." But he laughs as he says it. There is love in his face.

■   ■   ■

We both become angry once. He has been in a hospital bed for a week and is almost frantic with this compulsory restraint. It is almost unendurable to see him lying there, unable to speak, with a head full of words and intelligence. We visit him several times a day, and on one of these visits, when Majel leaves the room to talk to the doctor, he tries to get out of bed. "You can't do that, Gene," I say. *Star Trek: The Next Generation* is on the television.

"I can't . . . stay here. Let . . . me . . . up."

"No. I can't. But I'll go get a nurse."

The nurse comes in and tells him to lie down. He asks why. "You have to stay in bed," she says.

"That's not an answer to why," I tell her.

"You have to get well," she tells Gene.

He looks furious. Like a caged lion, he rattles the sides of his bed. "Let me up," he says again.

"Now, now—don't be like that. You have to stay in bed."

He is so outraged, so humiliated by this inane exchange, that he rolls his eyes in my direction like an injured animal.

"Can't you just explain it to him?" I ask.

She doesn't answer. She is essentially a kind person and tucks the covers securely around him. He emits a growl. "There, now," she says, patting him. "You be nice."

I feel his humiliation in silence. I am enraged—not at her, but at the fact that this reality exists. How can he be here, being patronized? It is outrageous.

"You see this TV show?" I point at the screen. "Well, this"—I point to Gene's shaved and wired head—"is where it came from—every idea, every dream—and *you aren't even speaking to him as a human being.*" I try not to raise my voice. "He isn't an idiot. *Talk to him,* for God's sake. *Explain.* And if you can't, go and get someone who can. This is a *person*—this is an intelligent man."

She looks at my face. "I'll go get a doctor," she says.

I wipe unexpected tears from my face and sit down.

There is a muffled, weary sound from the bed. "Thanks."

■　　■　　■

When the doctors arrive—and there are several of them—one, Louis Rosner, asks what the problem is. I explain. He gives Gene a full, complex, and detailed account of his current status and the reasons it is inadvisable for him to stand upright at this time. "So, you understand," he concludes, "why it is absolutely imperative that you stay put."

"Yes," Gene answers, "I *understand.*"

■　　■　　■

He is not as distressed about his inability to speak as others are on his behalf, he tells me later, when he is back home. That communication takes almost half an hour. "I just—think," he says. It seems to be sufficient for the time being. I tell him he is like Stephen Hawking. His face lights up.

"Hero," he says.

Eighteen months later, Stephen Hawking appears on the *Star Trek: The Next Generation* episode "Descent," playing himself as a historical figure whose brilliance changed the world. Everyone connected with this episode is honored, awed. Everyone thinks of Gene.

■　　■　　■

THE END

We talk about male bonding in science fiction before all this happens. I have just finished writing a series of papers on that theme. This finally leads us to Robert Heinlein's *Space Cadet.*

"I think people in science fiction open their minds— perhaps that's not it—open their consciousness to a lot—a lot of relationships," Gene says.

"Perhaps that's because in traditional science fiction, the protagonists are so often not functioning in society—they're on a spaceship or a distant planet, and as they get farther and farther away from the cultural requirements of their society, they just behave in a more . . . real manner. I'm not talking about homosexuality here, but just the bonds between people. They're the only ones out there, so they rely on each other to supply the human contact and emotional support that would have been spread around and colored by the conventions that no longer exist for them."

"Oh, yes—definitely. That definitely happens. But Bob Heinlein was also capable of creating female bonding—and many other kinds of bonding—and he lived longer than I have in a society that puts limits on how he can think about it. And I am able to think about it a little more broadly, but I am still more limited than, say, some of the people of my acquaintance who have had other experiences. But I have friends that I hug and kiss. I've always been a kisser—or I've always been forming into a kisser and a hugger."

. . .

The last time I ever saw Gene, I bent down and gave him a hug, and he took my hand and kissed it. And Sam Rolfe was with us and was very embarrassed. He didn't like that—not comfortable with men holding men. But Gene

had no problem with that at all, in public or anywhere—
oh, no. He was very affectionate.

—Christopher Knopf

▪   ▪   ▪

"Of course, you grew up in L.A., didn't you?" I say,
laughing.

He smiles back. "Yeah, but I also grew up in World War II—
in the Pacific and so on."

"Yes," I say doubtfully, wondering in what ways growing
up in a war could make one a hugger and kisser. He answers
the doubt in my face.

"Well, remember, I grew up into the man who created *Star
Trek*."

We both think about this for a while. I wonder out loud if
there were *Star Trek* impulses inherent in his genetic material. He does not think it a fanciful question. Later, when I
learn the circumstances of his birth, I do not think so either.
We both, as children, spent time sitting in grocery boxes,
dreaming of other worlds. He, some twenty-seven years
before me, propelled his grocery box through a thousand
galaxies. My destination was more defined: the "when you
wish upon a star" star seen each week in what was to me
then, and remains now, haunting poignancy, on *The Wonderful World of Disney*.

I searched for it every time my mother would allow me to
stay outside past dusk, I tell him.

"So you too love longing," he remarks, but does not pursue
it.

We find out from each other that we would lie awake at
night, as very young children, aching with yearning for what
we thought of as going *back* to the stars. "I used to cry about
it," we tell each other, and in the telling know no more need

be said. He piloted real airplanes around the real planet Earth, while I was walking home from kindergarten, puzzled by the ever-present horizon that always seemed like a barrier one was destined to escape. And we muse and reminisce as if we shared the same past, as if we were not a generation, a gender, and a world war apart. Two very new old friends, whose real heroes are fictional characters, and whose lives were both influenced by Robert Heinlein's *Space Cadet*.

■   ■   ■

"What is it about *Space Cadet* that makes it so important to you?" I ask when we have returned from our shared and separate pasts.

"I think it's just that—bonding. I find that sort of bonding among explorers very compelling. It means so much—has always meant so much—to me to know that great science fiction includes great human connection. It speaks to the socio-organism idea that we talked about earlier. *Space Cadet* is a very humane book. It deals with the problems not only of science—about space travel and technology and so on—but of the need we have to act in a conscious, responsible manner with all this technology. Of course it was written many years before space travel was really an actual problem, but the ideas contained within it are timeless. It made a great impression on me."

"Me too. Especially its code—the code the Patrol live by."

"Yes, I know, but I've forgotten exactly what it is. I remember thinking when I was creating *Star Trek* that our people would have a similar code—a band of brothers, wasn't it?"

■   ■   ■

In the *Star Trek: The Next Generation Writers' Guide*, under a section entitled "What Has Not Changed" (from the Original Series), the first item on the list is entitled "The Same

'Band of Brothers' Feeling" and states: "A large part of the success of the original *Star Trek* series is attributable to the fact that it was not a 'star' and 'co-star' series, but a family ensemble, in which the continuing characters felt great affection for each other. . . ."

I have *Space Cadet* with me during this discussion, and so read the appropriate passage aloud:

I welcome you to our fellowship. You come from many lands, some from other planets. You are of various colors and creeds. Yet you must and you shall become a band of brothers.

"Yes, that's it," Gene says. "Read the rest."

Some of you are homesick. You need not be. From this day on, every part of this family of planets is your home, each place equally.

"Each place, equally," Gene repeats.

Each living, thinking creature in this system is your neighbor—and your responsibility. You are about to take an oath by your own choice, as a member of the Patrol of this, our system. In time, you expect to become an officer of that Patrol. It is necessary that you understand the burden you assume. You expect to spend long hours studying your new profession, acquiring the skills of the spaceman and the arts of the professional soldier. These skills and arts you must have, but they will not make you an officer of the Patrol. . . . An officer in command of a ship of the Patrol, away from base, is the last of the absolute monarchs, for there is none but himself to restrain him. Many places where he must go, no other authority reaches. He himself must embody law and the rule of reason, justice, and mercy.

More than that, to the members of the Patrol singly and together is entrusted such awful force as may compel or destroy all other force we know of—and with this trust is laid on them the charge to keep the peace of the System and to protect the liberties of its peoples. They are soldiers of freedom.

It is not enough that you be skillful, clever, brave; the trustees of this awful power must each possess a meticulous sense of honor; self-discipline beyond all ambition, conceit, or avarice; respect for the liberties and dignity of all creatures; and an unyielding will to do justice and give mercy. He must be a true and gentle knight.[24]

I look at Gene. "Starfleet?" I ask.

"Starfleet, yes. That book had such a profound influence on me, as did Bob. There are so many, many ideas that we shared. He wrote many of them down before I did, but they were—have always been—in my heart."

"I notice something he said that you told me early in our acquaintance—"

"Friendship," he corrects me.

"Friendship. And that was that it was a frightening burden to know that you know the answers. Or must find them out for yourself."

"Yes, and that's why I reject religion."

"Yes, and that's why the paper I wrote on *Space Cadet* is subtitled 'The Monastic Journey in Space.'"

"It's not!"

"It is."

---

[24]*Space Cadet*, by Robert Heinlein, Random House: New York, 1948, pp. 45–46.

"I want to read it."

"Okay."

"*Space Cadet* is such a significant book for both of us," he says. "Perhaps in it, we meet, in the middle of your strange 'theology,' if that's the right word, and my agnosticism."

"With you staying carefully on your side of the line?"

"For the time being. If I find a different answer, when I have passed on, I'll let you know."

"You'll haunt me?"

"Yes."

.   .   .

The religious geniuses of all ages have been distin-guished by this kind of (cosmic) religious feeling, which knows no dogma and no God conceived in man's image . . . hence it is precisely among the heretics of every age that we find men who are filled with the highest kind of religious feeling and were in many cases regarded by their contemporaries as Atheists, sometimes also as Saints.

—*Albert Einstein*

.   .   .

There are a good many contradictions in that Heinlein code. It seems to say a man (person) must be everything: a warrior, a pacifist, a staunch individual, and a willing cog in the mechanism of a galactic socio-organism, a man who obeys laws and breaks them, creates his own and polices them. He must be friend to all and to none, because he must be impartial to all. He must walk the line between passion and reason, and never fall, lest he lose his footing forever. He must respect all gods, while honoring his own, renounce his home planet and be at home everywhere. The limits of space are his only boundaries, and the burden of freedom, his only responsibility. And above all, he must be a true and gentle knight.

When, in 1993, Gene is posthumously awarded the Robert A. Heinlein Memorial Award for Lifetime Achievement in Promoting the Goal of a Free Spacefaring Civilization, I will write Majel's acceptance speech of behalf of Gene. It is later published in *Ad Astra*, the magazine of the National Space Society. They give it a title: "A True and Gentle Knight."

There is another, deeper contradiction in *Space Cadet*, which I have sensed in Gene, and that is the conflict of what it means to him, personally, to be. Throughout our conversations, he has evidenced some distress at his inability to leap beyond the definition of manhood and into the wider realm of personhood. He has been crippled, he tells me once, by his own history as a male person in the twentieth century on Earth. His intimates are men. His heroes are men. And what *Space Cadet* is about, beneath its cosmic significance and ontological imperatives, is men, or rather, manhood. Its code, which touches us both on some mysterious symbolic level of the psyche, has something to do with metaphysics for me; for him, I am not sure. I ask him just for the record, but it does not matter. I am accustomed, by virtue of my age and particular experience, to investing an idea with a personal relevance, used to reading *person* in place of *man* whenever the reference is appropriate. I assume all women of my generation are, whether they choose now to object to it or not. *Space Cadet*, for me, is a book about the human—not gender—spirit.

In answer to my question, Gene makes a potentially explosive observation. He says that it is the virtues of manhood that will carry us into the future, and therefore, they are the virtues he upholds. What he means, of course, is that the attributes traditionally dubbed male—courage, resoluteness, detachment, independence, devotion to duty above personal concerns, a disregard for emotional or physical pain—are the vehicles that will transport us into the future. He does not need to be told that these traits are the property of humankind and not just males, but he is at a loss to assimilate them easily and naturally as female attributes in the pattern of life he has led as a male. Something inside him distrusts the reliability of this viewpoint. He has been a man too long.

We have a long and careful conversation about it. He is ashamed to regard himself as parochial, proud that he has not let the limitations of his own history prevent him from changing history for others. He reveals a pattern in this conversation—of monastic detachment, idealism, knighthood, courtly love (the essential ingredient of which is longing), the internal renunciation of the present, in which women richly, fully, properly spend their time, in favor of the future for which he says he feels responsible. He says, without saying it, that to admit women into his intimate circle is to be seduced into today—that experience is not for him, except momentarily. Apart from Majel, who may travel with him as a dream, he cannot incorporate any bonds within him that bind him to Earth—cannot allow himself any reasons to give up a relentless pursuit of the cause of being, in favor of being it. Women don't understand this, he says. Except, perhaps, nuns. He smiles at me and adds, oddly, mischievously, that he thinks he might like to have been a nun for a while. I dub him Sister Mary Gene. He knows he will be criticized for these statements, asks me to write about rather than transcribe them. It makes sense to me. What he says about women is not uncomplimentary. It is his own personal circumstance that drives him from them. They are what they are. As is he.

He talks a lot, during this elliptical conversation, about the fusion and fission of male and female. Somehow, in common with ancient mythologies, he feels that two genders are an evolutionary mistake. When I ask him what the limitations of androgyny are, he cannot answer me. He asks, "What is androgyny exactly?"

"It means neither male nor female. Both, I guess. Or maybe, not either."

"Well," he says thoughtfully, "I hope I'm not either."

■   ■   ■

In his treatment of the Gaan character, Gene describes the world from which he comes. It is called Uhl.

The most significant difference between Uhl and Earth life, perhaps even greater than their life structure variations, is the ways they replicate themselves. Here too, the early life on Earth and Uhl began in much the same way, with the early organisms of both worlds dividing themselves into identical halves. All life on Uhl still uses variations of that same system, although this world's more complex life-forms must join into one double-creature and exchange identities before parenthood is possible. Then, upon separating into individuals again, one or both of them are capable of increasing their species population by dividing into replica halves. Each individual gives and shares equally in all this, and any concept of male and female would be meaningless.

■   ■   ■

"I've learned to appreciate females very much," he goes on, "but I didn't start off appreciating them. I was a writer who believed that men were more logical than women. Now I don't think they're more logical; they may operate on principles of logic more. But I do not consider males mentally superior to women. Physically, perhaps.

"I am pleased with myself that I have evolved to appreciate women as much as men," he says, looking very pleased with himself indeed. "You see, it's not a matter of superiority or inferiority; it's a kind of difference. Their femaleness is not a sign of weakness—we have very powerful women on *The Next Generation*, but I can't involve Gene Roddenberry in their femaleness. Not in what I have to do. And that is probably a failing on my part."

He mixes metaphysics and sex and gender in a long and complex speech, from which I conclude he means that it is not because he is a man that he feels this way. It is because of the kind of man he is. Quixotic, Questor. Spock. He does not belong here. Nor will he stay much longer. Earth is no longer his home.

What *Space Cadet* really means to him is a chance to be a guardian of the human race, an opportunity to live out an ideal in a kind of cosmic monasticism. It is what led me to a place in which *to be* was a true objective; it is what led him to the creation of *Star Trek*, in which the same objective is implicit. In addition, he has found, in *Space Cadet*, an opportunity to be a true and gentle knight.

Gentleness is all I have known from Gene—gentleness and a certain archaic chivalry. At times, it seemed at odds with a man whose thoughts seemed to be entirely focused on the future, whose pursuits might not leave time for old-fashioned courtesy, and whose friends recount stories of his raucous, bawdy, daredevil, even immoral and unethical exploits. It does not seem consistent. But I never knew his outside personality, never saw him for more than a few moments in company with anyone save his intimates. Perhaps this gentleness was the result of all his former experience; perhaps he was originally that way. All I know is that when I brought this misgiving to his attention, he was mystified.

"But you are writing about me," he said.

"Yes . . ."

"This is me."

THE END

This is the last long conversation we will have. Tomorrow, he will have a stroke. From this point on, we will rely on fragments, references to former conversations, individual words—sometimes, a sentence or two. Tomorrow, he begins a new journey.

. . .

Sometime in the night, he cries out. He is not well, Majel tells me the next morning. At breakfast, he is unable to articulate clearly. We take him to the doctor. On the way, he is patient, smiling, gentle. I wait in the outer office while Majel and Gene are with the doctor. When they emerge, she tells me that he is being sent for a routine scan later that afternoon and asks me to go with them.

Just before that appointment, all the pipes in the house break and there is water everywhere. Majel asks me to take Gene to his second appointment while she deals with the crisis, and promises to make his favorite dinner. His driver brings the car to the front of the house, and we leave. He will not be back for weeks.

We are sitting in the second doctor's office. We do not speak. Gene's eyes are closed. He leans toward me slightly. "Find me," he whispers. We play our game to distract him from pain. I make up a lot of nonsense, which makes him smile. I know where he is, but am afraid to say it.

A receptionist asks him to sign a card. "Just sign your name there," she says.

He looks at me with something in his face I do not recognize. He writes nothing. After about a minute, he touches my arm. "My name?" he asks politely.

I look into his eyes, willing it to be a joke. Horror crawls up my back. My legs begin to shake. He waits patiently.

"Gene Roddenberry," I say.

"Oh, yes. Thank you." I help him write it down, help him

back to his seat, and use every ounce of energy I have not to cry. It is not enough. I lower my head. He takes my hand as two tears drop on his beautiful fingers. "Oh," he says softly, and closes his fingers. "I'll be all right."

This cannot happen. It can't. He was talking about laser technology yesterday. Eighteen hours ago. I will not believe it. The doctor comes out with a grave face. "Take him to the hospital *now*," he says. "Don't go home. Don't stop anywhere. Just go." He gives me a piece of paper. I call Majel from the car. It is a nightmare, I think; I will wake up—it's just the other side of dreams.

During the drive to the hospital he says one thing. "I *knew* it."

"Your name?"

"Yes," he says.

"I know you did, Gene. You just couldn't write it."

"Yes," he says. "Thank you."

■   ■   ■

It is this courteous, courageous, and self-contained demeanor that reveals so much about Gene Roddenberry to me. He is extremely ill. He is in severe pain. He never deviates from this behavior, never once complains. Majel meets us at the hospital, takes care of a thousand details. When it appears that he will have to go into an ambulance to make the short journey from one part of the building to another, she tells him she will go home—a few blocks away—and get his own things, so he will be more comfortable. "You stay with him," she says. "I'll be back in a few minutes."

■   ■   ■

In the ambulance, we must wait for a while. He holds my hand and keeps very still. After a while, he tugs at my hand.

"Where's . . . Majel?" he asks.

"She'll be back in a minute."

"Good."

He falls asleep for a few minutes. When he wakes up, he looks at me for a long time.

"I'm afraid," he says.

"I know, Gene."

He grips my hand. "I might die."

"No, I don't think so—not yet."

He closes his eyes. "Fear," he says with a sigh.

"The answer to my question."

"Yes."

I pat his hair with one hand. The other is still in his. "I just don't believe in nothing, Gene."

He smiles again, an odd, brave, grateful smile. "Good."

When he falls into a half-sleep again, I wonder where everyone is. It seems as though we have been there for hours. It is, in reality, only a few minutes.

"Majel," he says again, with his eyes still closed.

"Don't worry—she's on her way."

"No . . . I . . . find me."

I close my eyes, and find him. "That's not what you meant."

"No." He tugs on my hand. "Love her," he says, pulling me closer to him.

"I do."

He is very, very tired, and his next words come with effort.

"Never . . . leave . . . her."

I bite my lip until it bleeds. "No, of course not. Don't worry." I want so badly to pretend that I feel he is not dying. But I am not an actress after all. Not with him. He kisses my hand and falls asleep.

Majel arrives a few minutes later, takes one look at my face, and pinches me on the arm, hard. "He is going to be *fine*," she hisses. "Now *look* like it." She lets my arm go with a warning glance as he wakes up and sees her. He seeks her eyes for signs of his existence. The look on his face is akin to ecstasy. He opens his arms.

"Well, my darling," she says to Gene, cupping his face with her hands and kissing him. "What have you two been up to, to get yourselves into this situation?!"

■　　■　　■

Only a few days earlier, in that discussion about acting, Gene had asked me to tell him what I thought was the best performance I had ever seen a *Star Trek* actor give. This was it.

■　　■　　■

He lives for a few more weeks. During those weeks, we visit him in the hospital, make lists of words he can point to when he cannot speak, take him out to dinner, when he is well enough to come home. He has no trouble thinking. We talk a little. One day, he seems much better. He speaks in sentences.

"I'm sorry about the book," he says.

"Never mind," I tell him. "We'll get back to it when you're better." I feel I am being false, but Majel is nearby, and I do not wish to be pinched again. He looks at me steadily and knowingly. He has seen me look at him where he is, slightly adrift of his body, which now has a translucent quality I recognize from past experience.

"I have to die, you know," he says when Majel is out of earshot.

I do not answer him.

"I'm not afraid, now." He looks toward the door. "Take care of her. She doesn't understand. . . ."

"I know. I will."

"Promise?"

216

THE END

I nod my head. How assiduously they protect each other. There will be no "until death do us part."

"Go to the set. Find me."

"Gene . . ."

He will not listen. He issues instructions all day long.

Just before I leave to go home, I go into the bedroom to say good-bye. I embrace the fragile body in which there once lived a six-foot-three L.A. cop, a Pan Am pilot, a World War II hero, a Hollywood television producer, a legend, an enigma, a friend—and in which he is now barely present. "Come back often," he says. "Come back *soon*." As I walk out the door, he says, "I love you."

■　　■　　■

I never see him again.

Epilogue

. . .

Is there a portrait of Gene Roddenberry in all this? There
might be. It depends on the viewer. To those to whom a
portrait is an interpretation, a few lines sketched in the brief
passage of the time between life and death, between substance and shadow, yes. To those who expect a photographic
likeness, no, there is no portrait. The light will always be
wrong, the profile not sharp enough, the shutter speed not
quick enough to catch the face of a man who turns suddenly
to the window to catch a glimpse of an undiscovered star.

One will always wonder if he is the man at the Harvard
lectern, discoursing on the future of photoelectric cells, or
the man who dissects the symbology of acting, all the while
playing happily with the cast of characters inside himself—
becoming first one, then the other—in order to discover what
it means "to be." Or whether he is none of these people at all,
but a fictional persona of his own choosing. He is too quick
for the artist's brush, too still for the movie camera that seeks
a few seconds' summary in the face of the unknown. Was he
human? Yes. As human as every alien he created. Did he feel
he was a part of humanity? No. Not when I knew him. He felt

as alien as every human who walks this earth in his shell of flesh, "self-contained, separate . . . terribly lonely."[25]

The first day I met him, I asked him what one sentence he would like for an epitaph. Without hesitation, he replied, "He loved humanity."

■   ■   ■

And yet, when I look back, there was one evening in June when the world seemed to open up for him, for a few seconds, as Majel passed by. He looked at her, and then his eyes traveled to the purple evening sky. "You know, Yvonne," he said, "if I could just understand Majel, I think I could understand the whole of humanity."

---

[25]Spock/Kolos, "Is There in Truth No Beauty?," *Star Trek,* the Original Series, third season.

Acknowledgments

This edition of *The Last Conversation* was prepared with the attentive and capable assistance of Kevin Ryan and Margaret Clark at Pocket Books. Of those acknowledged in the original edition, Majel Barrett Roddenberry, Arthur C. Clarke, James H. Clark, the Editorial Department of the University of California Press, Russell Galen, William J. McClung, Robert H. Justman, and my family were the true facilitators of the manuscript.

I thank them all.

Herbert F. Solow, executive in charge of production for *Star Trek*, who hired Gene Roddenberry in 1964 and has since become my husband, best friend, and partner in all endeavors, I thank most profoundly for telling me the truth.